A Biological Brain
in a
Cultural Classroom
Second Edition

Robert Sylwester

A Biological Brain in a Cultural Classroom

Second Edition

Enhancing Cognitive and Social Development Through Collaborative Classroom Management

CORWIN PRESS, INC.
A Sage Publications Company
Thousand Oaks, California

For information:

Corwin Press, Inc.
A Sage Publications Company
2455 Teller Road
Thousand Oaks, California 91320
www.corwinpress.com

Sage Publications Ltd.
6 Bonhill Street
London EC2A 4PU
United Kingdom

Sage Publications India Pvt. Ltd.
B-42 Panchsheel Enclave
Post Box 4109
New Delhi 110 017 India

Printed in the United States of America

Library of Congress Cataloging-in-Publication Data

Sylwester, Robert.
A biological brain in a cultural classroom: Enhancing cognitive and social development through collaborative classroom management / Robert Sylwester.–2nd ed.
    p. cm.
Includes bibliographical references and index.
ISBN 0-7619-3810-9 (Cloth) – ISBN 0-7619-3811-7 (Paper)
  1. Classroom management-Psychological aspects.
  2. Learning-Physiological aspects. 3. Brain. I. Title.
LB3011.5 .S95 2003
371.102´4–dc21

                          2002154831

This book is printed on acid-free paper.

03   04   05   06   10   9   8   7   6   5   4   3   2   1

Acquisitions Editor:	Faye Zucker
Editorial Assistants:	Julia Parnell and Stacy Wagner
Copy Editor:	Gillian Dickens
Production Editor:	Melanie Birdsall
Typesetter:	C&M Digitals (P) Ltd.
Proofreader:	Theresa Kay
Indexer:	Michael Ferreira
Cover Designer:	Tracy E. Miller
Production Artist:	Sandra Ng Sauvajot

Contents

Preface

My original plan was to become a biologist, and so I focused on biology during my undergraduate years. Ecology interested me the most. My first postcollege job, however, was to teach 36 students in an eight-grade, one-room rural school. Since I also drove the bus, I was continuously with my age 6 through 14 students from the first pickup at 7:30 a.m. to the final drop-off at 4:00 p.m. The concept of a substitute teacher (let alone of an aide or custodian) didn't exist.

Overwhelmed, I came to peace with my situation by viewing it ecologically. I became fascinated by the related notions of a classroom as an ecological system of checks and balances and by a management focus on the logical consequences of behavior (rather than on punishment, the focus of my own schooling). I began a graduate program during my 9 years as an elementary teacher, but I veered from biology into education. Still, I increasingly focused on such biologically related educational issues as learning and behaving and on such ecological issues as space-time relationships and the distribution of power and resources in school. My doctoral dissertation focused on classroom management, a key ecological concept in education. Biological research focuses on organisms and their behavior, so I sought to discover how students view their own behavior—their view of what they do that annoys teachers, how teachers respond to such annoyances, and how fair and effective students consider teachers to be.

I discovered that even young students are keen observers of their situation. Well, why not? Their well-being during the school day depends on it. Most know more about their teachers than their teachers know about them because they only have to observe one teacher, while the teacher's observations are spread out among the entire class. I discovered that students consider fairness (the ecologically equitable distribution of authority, effort, and resources) to be a critically important component of school life.

I translated my dissertation research and management beliefs into two professional books early in my college teaching career. I then continued my interest in classroom management through journal articles and a graduate seminar I regularly taught for more than 25 years. Our understanding of stress (and its effect on behavior and misbehavior) and of the brain systems that trigger stress and process cognition increased dramatically during this period, and so my focus on the biological and ecological substrate of educational policy and practice intensified.

I also always spent a lot of time in schools—working with practicum students, observing student behavior. Most student projects in my classroom management seminar gathered and analyzed behavioral and opinion data from students (generally their own). These informal investigations solidified my belief that K–12 students know and feel more about classroom management issues than we often realize and that the worst-behaved students (from the teacher's perspective) often have the most astute opinions about what's going on. K–12 students may be right or wrong, informed or uninformed, but it's foolish for educators to be ignorant of and/or to ignore what students believe. If for no other reason, they outnumber us.

We've always used extrinsic rewards and punishments to prop up adult control of formal education, and we currently seem obsessed with the biologically quaint notion that we can precisely measure all the important forms of student learning and achievement—and in an increasingly competitive school environment, to boot. Furthermore, we're not of one mind about what the schools should teach.

I thus thought it might be a worthy enterprise at this point in my career to revisit what I focused on first in my career, to see if the recent biological discoveries and my professional experiences have anything helpful to say to the current and continuing dilemma about how best to manage formal education in a democratic society. That was the original impetus for this book.

In partial preparation, I reread my dissertation and my first two books—for the first time in decades. I was so proud of them when I wrote them, and I'm so thankful now that they're out of print. Still, the basic biological and ecological beliefs that began my professional and writing career continue to beat strongly within me: (1) students should learn how their own biological systems function (and especially their cognitive systems), now that that knowledge and its relationship to behavior is becoming available; (2) students should collaborate in classroom management decisions as much as possible; and (3) it's difficult at best to separate classroom management from instruction.

In a complex democratic society, participation means that a student's views will sometimes prevail and sometimes not, but students at least ought to have an opportunity to participate in decisions that affect them if they're old enough to attend school. How else could they develop the requisite participation skills needed by citizens in a democratic society? This book will explore the key dimensions of these beliefs and suggest how educators might collaboratively involve students in the search for and the direction of their own education.

I wrote the preface to the first edition of this book on the day after Labor Day in 1999. On that day 50 years earlier, I drove the bus and taught my 36 students for the first time. I'm revising the preface for this second edition on September 11, 2002—a year to the day after the World Trade Center bombing. Folks were optimistic in 1949 (4 years after World War II) that perhaps the world had tired of war, and geopolitical misbehavior would wane. It hasn't turned out that way, and we're now all apprehensive about the future. Educators can't control world events, but we can demonstrate the value of collaborative management and of supportive social interaction. And if enough of us successfully focus on these issues, perhaps the next generation will effect what past generations were unable to do. What else can educators do but teach and hope?

For me, it's been a long and satisfying trip from bus to word processor, from behaviorism to cognitive neuroscience—and I have many folks to thank: (1) the research biologists who are actually doing what I originally set out to do and who now are dramatically expanding our understanding of our brain, body, and culture; (2) the thousands of students from ages 6 to 60+ who told me much about themselves—and much about me that I hadn't realized; (3) the many fine editors and colleagues who helped me to find my own explanatory and interpretive voice; and (4) most important, my very loving and supportive wife and children and grandchildren who helped me to find, live, and enjoy my own life.

About the Author

Robert Sylwester is an Emeritus Professor of Education at the University of Oregon who focuses on the educational implications of new developments in science and technology. He is the author of several books and many journal articles. The Education Press Association of America gave him Distinguished Achievement Awards for his 1994 and 1995 syntheses of cognitive science research, published in *Educational Leadership*. He writes a monthly column in the acclaimed Internet journal *www.brainconnection.com*. He has made more than 1,300 conference and inservice presentations on educationally significant developments in brain and stress theory and research. He can be contacted at bobsyl@oregon.uoregon.edu.

CHAPTER ONE

The Cultural Foundations of Classroom Management

Schools continually confront the problem of determining how to insert about 100 pounds of student brain tissue (and accompanying bodies) into a 1,000–square foot classroom and then how to manage it appropriately over a 1,000–hour school year—biologically, ecologically, and developmentally. Since we educators attempt to enhance our students' ability to successfully confront life's challenges, you'd think that students would be pleased and appreciative of our efforts and so would participate joyfully in all classroom activities. Think again.

Classroom management is generally a major concern of beginning teachers (and also of their administrators), and most teachers consider it a difficult aspect of their assignment throughout their individual careers. Our profession has consequently developed an extensive classroom management literature. Some proposed programs focus principally on institutional values, such as maintaining a smoothly functioning, relatively quiet classroom; others focus on the developmental needs and/or legal rights of students; but most attempt to create a reasonable balance between institutional and personal needs.

In sum, though, the classroom management literature tends to view management as an element of school administration. The educators manage the students, who do the misbehaving. The reality, though, is that teacher and institutional misbehavior also occurs frequently in a school, and it's the cause of some (if not much) disruptive student misbehavior. So why do the educators get to make all the management decisions if they're part of the misbehavior problem?

The political goal is to run schools as inexpensively and efficiently as possible. The principal pressure on students is thus to perform, not to enjoy. Furthermore, the current politically powerful but biologically naive obsession with narrowly defined high-stakes standards and assessment programs that purport to precisely measure an imprecise brain simply exacerbates an already difficult situation.

To complicate things even more, educators must now also consider recent developments in the biological sciences that provide intriguing new perspectives of student and teacher behavior, misbehavior, and classroom management. These developments focus on such factors as innate predisposition, the relative interactive strengths of various neural systems, normal and abnormal fluctuations in hormonal and neurotransmitter levels, and stress mechanisms and processes. Knowing that a biochemical imbalance at least partially led to the inappropriate behavior of a teacher and/or student certainly doesn't solve the immediate management problem, but *knowing why* generally leads to *knowing how to*. New creative and compassionate approaches to classroom management will certainly emerge over time out of this knowledge, just as they emerged in the management of mental illness, once researchers and clinicians understood its biological substrate.

This book will thus focus on how our profession might begin to develop policies and practices that (1) incorporate a biological/ecological perspective into classroom management and (2) shift the focus of classroom management to that of a collaborative curricular laboratory for developing social skills. It won't suggest a handful of magic procedures for getting students to behave. It will rather provide the functional biological background information on behavior and suggest intriguing exploratory metaphors and activities that you will find useful as you begin to work with colleagues and students in the observation, discussion, and informal investigation of school behaviors that will lead you to a better understanding of social behavior and its management. Appropriate practical applications will certainly emerge out of such joint exploratory efforts. Some may emerge quickly, others years from now, but nothing will change if we don't begin the process.

We need to continually consider that classroom management isn't something totally separate from curriculum and instruction. Management issues tend to focus on behavior, but most school behavior is closely associated with curricular and instructional issues—which also have no magic solutions.

Compare a cook and a chef. Both can create very nutritious and delicious food, but they differ when things go wrong in preparation. For example, a recipe-driven cook who lacks an important ingredient in the recipe can't proceed without it, but a chef who understands the chemistry of ingredients and cooking processes can imaginatively substitute for the missing ingredient. Similarly, *cook-teachers* can successfully follow established management procedures, but they're limited in their ability to improvise when the procedures don't work. Conversely, *chef-teachers* understand both behavior and procedures, and so they can successfully improvise when conditions require it. This book is thus for *chef-teachers* and *apprentice chef-teachers* who want to get beyond the recipe orientation that has dominated classroom management for decades.

So as you read on, repress (at least slightly) our profession's almost innate tendency to seek immediate practical applications of new developments. Useful applications generally don't immediately emerge from major scientific developments. The DNA code was discovered in 1953, but most genetic engineering has occurred during this past decade. Cloning didn't emerge until 1997, and stem cells were discovered at the turn of the century. Furthermore, it's quite a trip from the tightly controlled variables of cognitive science laboratory research to messy classroom research, where the variables bounce off the walls.

Practical applications? What are the practical applications of an infant? Infants are wet, noisy pets, at least 20 years from a clear sense of how they will turn out. What we do with infants is observe them carefully and nurture them. We try out such things as music lessons and playing with balls if we note interest and ability, but we don't make wild promises about their accomplishments (except perhaps in family letters). As childhood merges into adolescence, real interests and abilities become clearer, and we then invest more heavily and decisively in potential *practical applications*.

Similarly with the brain sciences—in reality still in their infancy (but growing rapidly). It's a time to put our energy into getting acquainted with this *scientific infant* that will change our professional lives—to observe, explore, and nurture. Our discoveries about our own children don't generally surprise us because we've provided them with their *genes* and their *jeans*. Similarly, many discoveries from the brain sciences don't surprise us either because we educators have been working with a room full of brains for a long time, and although we may not completely understand neural networks and neurochemicals, we do know a lot about how minds and bodies function. Call it folklore knowledge if you wish, but our professional instincts have generally served us well. They thus provide us with a sense of competence in our ability to go from where we are (in our understanding of classroom behavior) to where we might be (in our understanding of the biology of behavior).

So for now, just relax with the broad concept of classroom management (as difficult as it may be to relax with such an emotionally charged issue). Realize that we're in this for the long haul. Think about how current management practices emerged and how you came to your own beliefs about behavior management. Let your mind fluctuate between what happens within the natural world and the classroom environment. Note similarities and differences. Consider how you might use things you learned in one environment to enhance life in the other. Mostly, though, realize that the base of our professional knowledge of behavior management is now shifting from folklore to scientific knowledge, from coerced student behavior to collaborative decision making—and that the revolution is occurring on our watch.

It's occurring on our watch because (as suggested above) so much of what we now know about the biology of our body and brain has occurred during the past decade, amazing as that might sound. So it's almost a matter of our profession flying blind—trying to determine what to do about scientific and related cultural developments while they're still occurring.

I firmly believe that the collaborative exploration of what to do is much more exciting for a teacher and class than being told what to do—but if you really prefer a prescriptive book that explicitly tells you how to manage your classroom, this book's probably not for you.

To better understand the emerging 21st-century biological, cultural, and institutional revolution that is the focus of this book, it might be useful to begin with a bit of historical perspective from another educational revolution related to classroom management that occurred at the beginning of the 20th century. The adage is that those who ignore history are doomed to repeat it. It's a cultural development that might be instructive on how we might effectively proceed in guiding the next century's revolution.

DEMOCRACY AND EDUCATION

In retrospect, it seems such an obvious idea. Why, then, did it take so long for someone to think of it and so much longer for people to accept and incorporate it into our schools?

By the beginning of the 19th century, the U.S. Constitution had codified the basic principles that were to define and govern our representative democracy. But it took almost 100 years for a dominant voice to argue that the policies and practices that schools use to instruct and manage students should demonstrate the democratic principles that future voters must master. We're a social species living in a democratic society, and the knowledge and skills that intelligent citizens need to function effectively in that setting aren't innate. They must be explicitly taught and continuously experienced.

John Dewey's *School and Society* was published in 1899 and *Democracy and Education* in 1916. Dewey built on the previous work of others, such as the European educators Johann Pestalozzi and Frederich Froebel, but he became the 20th century's powerful American voice in the educational revolution.

Rereading his books, it all seems so logical. Why wouldn't a fledgling democratic society demand that its public schools be laboratories for democratic behavior—tuned to the cultural needs and abilities of students? Why use the 12,000 hours that K–12 students spend in school to demonstrate the competing authoritarian societal perspective that the founders of the United States rejected in the war for independence? One explanation is that although our nation's strength and success came from its creative and entrepreneurial spirit, we also needed a large, compliant workforce that would follow orders and stay *on task*—behaviors that authoritarian school management practices would help develop. It's a perspective that would appeal to business-oriented school boards.

Still, one would think that Dewey's ideas for participatory classroom management would have been enthusiastically embraced and instituted in a democracy, and in one way they were. The Progressive Education Movement led to a wide range of enthusiastic implementation strategies (such as the Gary Plan, the Dalton Plan, and the Winnetka Plan) that were widely hailed. I was born in 1927, and so I went to school during the period when these new approaches had an opportunity to become integral to the schools. Unfortunately, my schools, like most other schools at the time, didn't function on democratic principles. Far from it. We didn't even explore *representative* democratic values. It's not that they were bad schools, but democracy was something we studied in civics class, where we learned to write down how our total government was organized—but we didn't learn how to democratically organize our small class-room community.

By mid-century, when I entered the education profession, Progressive Education was in serious decline—severely buffeted by its critics. In 1938, when he was 79, John Dewey published *Experience and Education,* a somewhat poignant title for a book in which he analyzed what went wrong with his dream to incorporate democracy into education.

To simplify a complex issue, Progressive Education tried to do too much too quickly; it didn't effectively provide teachers with the knowledge they needed to incorporate the ideas, allowing its critics to redefine the movement and then criticize their own definition of it. These same factors led to problems that other 20th-century educational movements experienced, such as the science, math, and social science programs of the 1960s and 1970s; Values Clarification Programs; and the Free School Movement.

The interesting thing is that now, at the beginning of the 21st century, many of Dewey's curricular, instructional, and management ideas have quietly been incorporated into American schools. It's taken 100 years after the movement began, which occurred 100 years after the Constitution was in place! We could appropriately ask why it took so long.

21st-Century Challenges

This book will argue that our profession is currently at a related transformational state. A biological science revolution has been under way for some time—with, as indicated above, a major escalation during this past decade. Furthermore, it might shortly explode with important new perspectives of what it means to be human at the cellular and systems levels. For example, scientists are currently immensely interested in the development of a comprehensive brain theory that will be of the scientific magnitude of $E = MC^2$, in that it will spark a revolution in the brain sciences at the beginning of this century that will be analogous to the revolution in the physical sciences that Albert Einstein's relativity theories sparked at the beginning of the past century. It may profoundly alter our view of ourselves, as democracy altered our view of society.

Such a global brain theory will inevitably lead to the emergence of the 21st-century versions of such folks as John Dewey, Jean Piaget, and B. F. Skinner—who will translate the biological theories into teaching, learning, and classroom management theories. And why can't you or one of your students become that person?

Educators should thus begin now to explore how best to respond to the biological science revolution. It won't go away if we just ignore it. This exploration should include studying the errors of previous failed movements that sought to transform education, as well as identifying educationally significant cognitive science developments that will play important roles in the educational theory that will emerge.

And as if the biological revolution isn't enough to keep our profession busy, a parallel revolution is occurring in computer technology—which has gone through three separate revolutions in the 30+ years since the silicon chip was developed: from mainframe computer to personal computer to the Internet. And if you think that that's the end of that revolution, dream on! Imagine the classroom management issues that computers will raise as they become more integral to classroom activity.

In *Experience and Education,* Dewey (1938) made a retrospective examination of the Progressive Education Movement, the dominant educational movement of the 20th century. Our immediate task is to begin a prospective exploration of the biological science and computer technology revolutions—which may well spark the dominant educational movement of the 21st century. It took almost 200 years for democratic values to be generally assimilated into classroom life. Let's hope that the biological science and computer technology developments begin to be generally incorporated into schools within the early years of the 21st century.

As suggested above, the exciting thing is that this is occurring on our watch, and so today's educators get to participate in the beginnings of all of the revolutionary excitement, turmoil, decisions, projects, plans, failures, and successes. Or else we can sit back and let others do it. If you work with colleagues who plan to choose the latter approach, encourage them to take early retirement, and so open up their professional spot for someone who will get involved. And don't criticize the educators of the past century for foot dragging if you similarly drag your 21st-century feet.

One never knows how a revolution will evolve. Could Albert Einstein have predicted the mid-century dropping of atomic bombs and the end-of-the-century video games? Atomic energy and the electronic revolution both emerged out of his theories. The Chinese word for *stress* has two characters. One means danger; the other means opportunity. Expect both within this emerging revolution in educational policy and practice.

Cultural and technological changes occur either *top-down* or *bottom-up.* Top-down means that an organization (such as a corporation or government) decides to change something and then simply decrees the change. Legislative decisions are a good example of how the process unfolds in government. The change gets implemented via majority vote, but it generally takes court cases and subsequent legislative tinkering before a major top-down change achieves real political consensus.

Bottom-up changes also begin with someone's idea. If it's a good idea, it will gradually and informally spread—otherwise it will disappear. The good ideas also tend to change in an almost Darwinian manner as they spread. An innovative idea may eventually achieve widespread use, but no one person or group will generally have completely designed its final state. No one *owns* it, and no one can regulate it.

The current standards/assessment movement is a good example of a legislatively mandated top-down innovation. Folks have tinkered with it for years, but it's achieved no widespread political consensus about its value or execution, and educators who are expected to implement it are among its most severe critics. Top-down innovations generally require coerced continued regulation and enforcement and often breed hostility.

Two excellent recent examples of very successful bottom-up innovations are rock music and the Internet. Rock music didn't begin in school music programs (which tended to focus on playing notes that dead guys composed). Young people wanted to play guitars and improvise, and since school music programs didn't focus on either, they played in garages and basements. The adult society was appalled at the music because it seemed that most rock groups knew only three chords—and loud. But one could appropriately ask why the school music programs hadn't taught them about guitars and composition and improvisation if they wanted it *done right.* Rock music thus developed according to its own rules, and if someone today objects to the music and lyrics, that's just too bad. The adult society doesn't *own* rock music and its variants and therefore can't control it.

The Internet began similarly. Folks initially simply wanted to develop a simple inexpensive procedure to connect scholars and researchers. That concept expanded rapidly. Thousands of nerds intent on expanding and simplifying the system gradually and informally merged their creative efforts into the Internet and all the marvelous communication capabilities it has. And the nice thing again is that no one owns it or can tax or easily regulate it. Rock music and the Internet are thus popular democracy at its innovative best.

So don't complain if current school policies and practices frustrate you. Begin a bottom-up revolution within your own classroom or school, and nurture it to enhance its further growth. The multiple intelligences movement, cooperative learning, and portfolio assessments are examples of such emerging successful bottom-up educational innovations. It can and has been successively done.

COLLABORATIVE CLASSROOM MANAGEMENT

Classroom management provides the best venue for initiating a major bottom-up educational change. It isn't part of the high-profile curricular areas or of the politically charged state standards/assessment program, and it occurs continuously throughout the school day. Furthermore, like parenting, folks generally realize that there's no single way to do it. Classroom management thus provides teachers with a great opportunity to become subversive under the educational radar screen!

A collaborative classroom management model also offers the best venue for inserting the exploration of important social skills into the school experience. As indicated earlier, school provides a continuing 12,000-hour laboratory experience with serial sets of nonkin who have different values, interests, and abilities. It's the only such broad, extended opportunity young people have to explore social development. To have mastered collaborative skills in a democracy is especially important when political allegiances are evenly divided. For example, the 1999 close and contested U.S. presidential election pushed democratic integrity and restraint to the edge. What a tragedy it is to continue to squander such an opportunity for student civic development on an authoritarian classroom management model.

These factors enhance the constant nonthreatening exploration of collaborative classroom management possibilities. Thousands of teachers and students imagining and trying out new ideas and sharing them with others will eventually develop creative breakthroughs that will spread personally and electronically through the profession. Think of all the innovations in computer software that emerged in recent years as folks tinkered until they found a better way to do something.

Don't be dissuaded by those who see collaborative classroom management as an abrogation of professional responsibility. Remind them that the U.S. war for independence was fought to ensure participatory governance and that concept ought to permeate management wherever and however possible in our society. Collaboration doesn't mean a license to run amok. Democracies do have regulations and sanctions.

To those who tell you that students will misbehave if we don't control them, ask if their students always behave now. Remind them also that a democracy is characterized as much by disagreement as by agreement. Our country has learned how to agree and disagree on governmental management issues without being unduly disagreeable, and classroom life can function similarly if we commit to that goal.

Misbehavior isn't necessarily negative. Misbehavior is to a classroom what pain is to a body. Pain is a diagnostic system that evolved in our body to keep our brain informed about the location and nature of potentially dangerous events (such as damage to a foot, although the rest of the body may be OK). Much classroom misbehavior is similarly diagnostic. Acting-out students are informing the teacher that the lesson isn't working with them (although it may be fine and fun for the rest of the class). That's useful, albeit often distressing information for the teacher. Citizen protests and demonstrations are similarly stressful to political leaders, but it's folly to view them only in negative terms or to ignore or repress them.

It's also not a given that learning can only occur in smoothly functioning, relatively quiet settings. Small children easily master complex video games—and such electronic environments are noisy and confusing. Adults are similarly fascinated by sporting events in which players have to think clearly and quickly in noisy, chaotic situations. This doesn't suggest that classrooms should be continually noisy and chaotic but rather that we probably ought to begin to think *out of the box* about the range of potentially positive classroom conditions that students should experience as they learn.

It's important, when contemplating a collaborative classroom management model, to realize that it's not the perfect solution to all management problems. For example, while *diagnostic* pain and misbehavior are useful, *chronic* pain and misbehavior aren't. Students who have continuing disruptive behavior problems may not relate easily to a collaborative model, but the adult versions of such students often don't relate well to their democratic responsibilities either. Democratic societies have coercive systems for such folks (prison being the adult version of childhood *time-out*). A teacher using a collaborative management model will certainly reprimand and punish students on occasion if they behave in a physically dangerous or culturally inappropriate manner. Democracies have both collaborative legislatures and coercive police.

The problem with an authoritarian model is that it's designed principally around the misbehavior of a small number of the students in a class. Most students relate reasonably positively to school. An authoritarian model requires the many students who are cooperative to operate under restrictions needed because of the uncooperative few. A collaborative management model focuses on the developmental needs of the many students who cooperate and deals separately if necessary with the few who don't.

I indicated earlier that the authoritarian management model probably emerged in part because our society needed a compliant workforce. The 19th and 20th centuries were industrialized, and much of our huge country's energy was expended on manufacturing and moving objects. Workers mastered a trade and often stayed with a company for many years.

The 21st century begins differently. Many in my own extended family design and move information rather than objects. Many don't *go* to work but rather work (on computers) at home or at least removed from the building where their employer is located. And many are self-employed. Those who work for someone else don't expect to stay with one employer throughout their career. I expect that your family circle is similar. What this suggests to me is that young people today need to learn not only how to be reasonably compliant but also how to become self-reliant. They don't need to be told what to do but rather need to learn how to become self-starters. They need to learn how to manage their energy, space, time, and movements within biological limitations and cultural expectations. For all these reasons, a collaborative classroom management model is an old idea whose time has truly and finally come.

So begin exploring collaboration wherever you're comfortable, and follow your own trajectory. Share what you're doing with other educators, and try out ideas that you get from them. No bureaucracy can stop thousands of educators (or budding musicians or computer nerds) intent on improving the current system. Don't be discouraged that bottom-up changes take time. Today's computers and the Internet (and rock music, for all that) are considerably different from what they were even 5 years ago. Realize that we're in this for the long haul. Recall John Dewey's regret that he tried to do too much too fast.

This book will help you begin, and Chapters 4 through 8 will focus specifically on the dynamics of a collaborative classroom management model. On the other hand, an exploration doesn't need a manual and explicit directions. All it needs is your strong desire to venture into something different and the collaborative imagination to figure out how to do it.

My journey down this path began when I was a sixth-grade teacher. Derek was a bright student who contributed much to the class. At the end of the year, he told me that he had enjoyed the year and that I had been a good teacher. He then smiled and continued, "You always let us vote on things, and we always voted the way you wanted us to vote."

I thanked him, but I was devastated later when I thought about what he had said. I hadn't realized until that moment how I had manipulated my students all year (and during prior years). My policy was to encourage class discussion of the issue at hand and then, before they voted on it, to summarize the various positions expressed. Derek was smart enough to realize that I typically (and probably unwittingly) biased the vote through my summary. He wasn't angry because he generally agreed with me, but he let me know that he knew what I was doing—even though I evidently didn't realize it.

What I was doing, of course, had little to do with developing democratic skills in my students. Rather, I was teaching them how to be influenced by celebrity endorsements in advertising.

From then on, I asked the students who held a position on an issue to summarize their position prior to our vote. So I learned something. You will too.

CHAPTER TWO

The Biological Foundations of Classroom Management

Chapter 1 focused on the issue of the cultural needs of a social species in a democratic society. It argued that young people need extended experience with the challenges of interdependent life with nonkin—and that participating in collaborative classroom management activities during their school years would develop the requisite social knowledge and skills.

The late 20th-century surge in biological discovery poses a second important educational issue. This development will require 21st-century schools to incorporate much more biology into the curriculum to prepare students for the profound moral, ethical, legal, cultural, and economic issues that are already emerging out of these scientific discoveries. Today's third graders will be voters in 10 years, expected to make informed decisions as they vote for candidates or on ballot initiatives related to complex issues in genetics and the brain sciences. It's one thing for scientists to discover how to manipulate genetic and cognitive systems, and it's quite another thing to know whether they should do it. Responsible voting on such issues requires at least a functional understanding of the underlying scientific base.

It will be difficult to insert more biology into the curriculum. Our profession is currently much more oriented to the social and behavioral sciences than to the natural sciences. Except for secondary school science teachers, most teacher education students major in the social sciences and tend to have a very limited academic preparation in biology. Furthermore, it will be difficult to insert the coursework in chemistry, biology, and cognitive neuroscience that a 21st-century teacher will need into an already packed teacher preparation program.

It's not a hopeless enterprise if we begin informally. The long-term strategy is to gradually enhance teacher and student understanding of biological functions and systems. Biology fortuitously exhibits striking parallels at various levels of organization. Processes that organize and regulate functions at cellular levels are related to processes that regulate similar functions in the entire organism and also in social systems. This suggests a functional relationship between the management of a body and classroom—a body enclosing interactive organs, a classroom enclosing interactive inhabitants.

It's an intriguing idea. A collaborative classroom management model is an ideal 21st-century venue for developing important social and democratic knowledge and skills, and it's also an excellent venue for helping teachers and students to study their own biological systems and processes. A two for one bottom-up innovation!

Let's begin with an introduction to biological inquiry, followed by a nontechnical functional introduction to key management-related concepts in biology. Chapter 3 will focus on the organization of our brain, and Chapters 4 through 8 will suggest how you might use this information to help your students collaboratively manage your shared classroom and also to better understand their own cognitive processes.

THREE FORMS OF BIOLOGICAL INQUIRY

The recent explosion of new biological knowledge was sparked by three areas of inquiry that are now combining to help explain the biology of behavior.

Genetics. Genetics focuses on the processing systems that regulate cell activity and division. Our knowledge escalated with the 1953 discovery of DNA, the biological coding system (for protein synthesis) that validated the genetic principles Charles Darwin had proposed about

100 years earlier (Calvin, 1996a, 1996b). With its powerful theoretic and research base, genetics is simply exploding with major advances in genetic engineering. Scientists have now completed their mapping of the entire human genome of perhaps 30,000 genes—a large number being dedicated to organizing and regulating our brain.

Knowing the location and sequence of all the human genes will profoundly affect the diagnosis and treatment of various genetically related diseases and many emotional, attentional, and learning disabilities that affect school policies and practices. As indicated above, the advances in gene manipulation will also carry a load of cultural baggage that we'll have to deal with—including issues that we can't yet imagine.

How will we manage disruptive behaviors that emerge out of strong innate predispositions? How should today's curriculum prepare students to deal with the medical, educational, judicial, and religious issues in genetics that they will confront as (hopefully) informed citizens a decade or more from now? How many current educators have the functional understanding of DNA, genetic engineering, and the issues that surround them to create such curricula? Practical solutions to these and related issues will certainly emerge in the years ahead (Sylwester, 2001).

Imaging Technology. Imaging technology monitors the operation of various body-brain systems—creating computerized representations of various body-brain properties, such as our blood flow patterns, electromagnetic fields, and chemical composition. Dramatic advances in functional magnetic resonance imaging (fMRI) technology have attracted the most recent attention. fMRI can currently create a three-dimensional computerized representation of an entire brain within seconds. Since the process can be repeated immediately, scientists can observe various changes in brain activity over the period of time that an individual carries out a cognitive task, a remarkable advance in our ability to directly observe and interpret normal brain behavior. And such technologies will certainly become faster and more powerful.

Furthermore, less invasive advances in imaging technology will lead to the eventual solution of current limitations that require the individual to lie immobile in a claustrophobic laboratory setting. These advances suggest that educational researchers could begin to use simpler imaging technologies relatively soon. Costs and complexity have thus far focused the use of imaging technologies on medical problems and not on the curricular, instructional, and assessment problems that concern us (Davis, 1997; Gevins, 1997; Posner & Raichle, 1994).

The 66 doctoral dissertations I've advised during my university career gathered data through such tools as questionnaires, observation, and literature analysis. We did reasonably well with what we had, but it's mind-boggling to imagine how much this next level of research capability will do to increase our biological understanding of the educative process and the procedures we use to manage it.

Evolutionary Psychology. Evolutionary Psychology is an important (somewhat hybrid) area of scholarship that has emerged during the past quarter of a century to focus on the properties that unite (rather than separate) the human family. *Human nature* is probably a useful descriptive term. Insights from Evolutionary Psychology have led to thoughtful explorations of why we do the things that we do—such as to develop cooperative communities, rear our children in a nurturing family environment throughout an extended childhood, develop technologies, and support the arts and religious organizations. Barkow, Cosmides, and Tooby (1992) provided the initial impetus, but others have recently written thought-provoking books on various aspects of the topic (Pinker, 1997; Premack & Premack, 2003; Ridley, 1996; Wilson, 1998; R. Wright, 1995).

Evolutionary Psychology will be problematic for some since it scientifically explores areas that have previously been the sole purview of theologians and philosophers. Evolutionary Psychology looks more to our biological roots than to the powerful belief systems that have emerged within various cultures. Educators have been only moderately successful in dealing with curricular conflicts over Darwinian developmental principles during the past 150 years, and the final accommodation, alas, is still down the road. How will we work it out in a democratic spirit that seeks to construct bridges rather than walls? We don't want to imply to young students who aren't yet capable of judging the validity of complex issues that their parents (on either side of the issue) are wrong in their beliefs.

We thus see the recent convergence of three important interrelated fields of scholarship—one focusing on cells, one on brains, and one on human societies. What emerges from their combined work is the set of basic concepts that can guide our exploration of the biology of behavior. Since they'll provide the context for much of the rest of the book, let's begin by informally examining them, constantly seeking parallels between biological life and classroom life.

KEY BIOLOGICAL CONCEPTS

Our body and brain are awesomely complex, but they also have an elegant simplicity about them. Thus, it's possible to begin to explore the biology of classroom management by focusing on a relatively small number of key concepts rather than on a welter of scientific facts and technical terms.

An Integrated Bodybrain Tuned to Our World

At the most fundamental biological level, we have the innate capability to function effectively within the limited natural space/time world that we inhabit. We use renewable stores of energy to move about in our search for resources and to avoid dangers. Thus, space, time, energy, movement, and range are major elements in human life—and not surprisingly, also in classroom life (as Chapters 4-8 will explore).

Body and brain? Scientists have now moved from a former separation of body and brain to a more integrated body-brain concept. For example, our immune and endocrine gland systems were formerly (but are no longer) considered as totally separate from our brain, and scientists now know that hormonal and other body systems profoundly affect our emotional life. This book will thus use the term *bodybrain* when it's difficult to separate body and brain. Recall that John Dewey suggested a century ago that we should educate the *whole child.* Comfortable furniture and clean air thus become classroom management issues when we think of the biology of classroom management.

When we focus especially on our brain's properties, scientists now know that we have a *social plastic* brain and an intellect that is *dynamic* and *distributed.* These three cognitive properties pose important classroom management challenges to educational leaders who wish to tune educational policy and practice to our bodybrain's biological capabilities and limitations.

A Social Plastic Brain

At the cellular level, the numbers are immense. Our brain has 100 billion neurons and a trillion glial support cells that combine to carry out our brain's various processing tasks. The neurons are so highly interconnected that any neuron is only a few neurons away from any other neuron (much as any of the world's billion telephones is only a few key taps away from any other phone). A multitude of neurons is thus involved in any cognitive action.

How does a brain organize its trillion-plus cells for effective action? At the major systems level, our brain is composed of (1) a subcortical area (the brainstem and surrounding systems) whose collection of pea- to walnut-shaped *modular* structures innately regulate many basic brain processes that look inward to our survival, emotional, and nurturing needs and, above it, (2) the large six-layer sheet of deeply folded neural tissue called the cortex. The cortex encompasses 85% of our brain, and it processes learned rational logical behaviors that look outward to the time/space world we inhabit.

The cortex is composed principally of hundreds of millions of highly interconnected hair-thin (100-neuron) minicolumns that extend vertically through the six cortical layers (called the gray matter). Each minicolumn is specialized to process a very specific unit of information (such as a horizontal line or a specific tone). One hundred adjacent minicolumns combine into a unit to form a macrocolumn (about the thickness of the lead in a pencil), which can process more complex functions related to the minicolumns it incorporates (perhaps to help differentiate between the cello and flute version of a tone). Thousands of related macrocolumns form one of the some 50 anatomically distinct areas that each hemisphere contains (Calvin, 1996a, 1996b). Think of the entire cortex as our library, the columns as books, and the some 100 distinct areas as the various *library* areas (that contain information on history, science, etc.).

Figure 2.1 is a side view illustration of the columnar organization of the six-layer cortex. To simplify things, only a few of the 100 neurons in a column are included. The short finger-like *dendrite* extensions from a cell body bring information from other neurons into the cell, and the single long *axon* (which sends information to other neurons) extends down the column through the cellular layers into the white matter, a dense web of axon connections beneath the gray matter. The axons eventually leave the white matter to connect with neurons in a related nearby column or to project into another brain area.

So think of a 100-neuron column (gray matter) as containing the information in a 100-page book and the axonal white matter as the

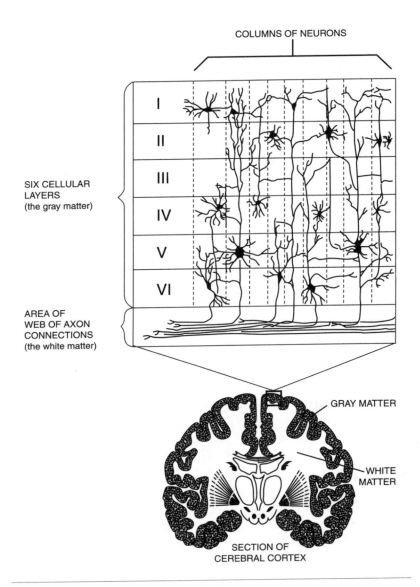

Figure 2.1   Schematic Side View of the Cortex

bibliography that connects the information in one book to other books.

Thus, discrete columnar brain areas and systems process basic limited cognitive functions. These are incorporated into larger, specialized, widely distributed but highly interconnected areas and systems that collaborate on complex cognitive tasks. For example, our visual system has about 30 separate columnar subsystems that process such visual properties as shape, depth, color, quantity, and movement. The subsystem that responds to the color red processes it on every red object we see, and the subsystem that responds to circular shapes processes balls, CDs, tires, donuts, and so forth. Several of these subsystems will combine to process our perception of a single red ball rolling across a table. Our brain is thus functionally similar to an interactive collaborating social system.

Two simple metaphors will help your students understand the division and organization of our brain's hundreds of processing systems, many of which are innately dedicated to a specific important task—and most of which aren't active at any given time.

A Library Metaphor. Think of how certain library shelves are assigned to a given category of books—fiction in one library area, science in another, and so on. A student would generally gather information from several books in a given area while preparing a report on that topic and would ignore library areas and books unrelated to the research topic.

Important library topics have more shelf space devoted to them, but the library's shelves can be reorganized to accommodate an expanding collection of books in a category. Dedicated (or modular) neuronal systems can similarly recruit neurons from less dedicated surrounding areas if they need more power to process their task. We can observe this developing spatial inequality in the larger amount of motor cortex space dedicated to coordinating movement in a person's dominant arm/hand as compared to the other, or in the expansion of neuronal space devoted to left-hand digital capabilities when a right-handed person becomes a violin student (Elbert, Pantex, Weinbruch, Rockstroh, & Taub, 1995).

A Kitchen Metaphor. A kitchen is a room where food is received, stored, and processed (and a brain similarly receives, integrates, and stores information arriving from inside and outside the body). A kitchen is filled with provisions and utensils suitable for a wide variety of menus, but most aren't being used at any given time. A cook planning to cook carrots uses only a peeler, knife, pan, water faucet, seasonings, and stove—not potatoes, the toaster, or other kitchen provisions or utensils. A recipe is a record of which kitchen provisions and utensils are used to prepare the food (and as indicated above, a brain scan similarly records which brain areas are involved in an activity).

In a kitchen, a few key ingredients and utensils are used in almost all food production activity—food staples such as salt and onions, as well as utensils for cutting and heating (and a few key brain systems and functions are similarly central to much of what we do).

Finally, kitchens often contain dull knives, broken equipment, and under- or overripe food that can affect the proper preparation of a menu (and our brain can contain immature and malfunctioning systems that reduce the overall effectiveness of cognitive activity).

We live in a complex environment, and so we must also effectively respond to challenges beyond our innate capabilities. When we don't *know* how to respond, we have to *figure out* what to do. Goldberg (2001) reported that many such learned behaviors are processed in our large cortex via a gradient principle, in which many small, massively interconnected, and highly interactive systems gradually develop initial decisions and behaviors that successfully respond to novel challenges. These responses are often only good enough to ensure our survival, but they become quite efficient with repeated use.

This ability to adapt neural systems to environmental demands is called *plasticity,* and it's obviously central to what occurs through teaching and learning. Plasticity researchers have discovered that a stimulating social environment is a major enhancing factor in the physical development of a brain (Diamond & Hopson, 1998).

This modular/gradient system of brain organization means that recent dramatic advances in brain imaging technology can help scientists to identify highly specific brain areas that don't function properly in children with a specific cognitive handicap. Locating such a neurological deficit is the first step in solving the problem.

The Fast ForWord (Scientific Learning Corporation, 1997) program emerged out of research discoveries of specific aural processing deficits in children who were seriously delayed in learning to speak and to comprehend speech. The Fast ForWord program has achieved remarkable results through its use of stimulating video game technology that speeds up the child's aural processing ability.

This may well be the technological prototype for future interventions that require extensive practice to speed up, slow down, or rewire the various adaptable neural systems involved in a disability. Since students who master language skills with difficulty often (understandably) create classroom behavior problems, such interventions may lead to a major reduction in some kinds of classroom management problems (Schwartz and Begley, 2002).

Our profession has become interested in theories of multiple intelligences in recent years, and these theories are based on our brain's modular/gradient organization. That the location of most neural systems, subsystems, and interconnections involved in various intelligence categories has yet to be precisely identified doesn't diminish the reality of a *social* brain as the biological substrate of the theories. It's an important concept for educators who accept any theory of multiple intelligences—and imaging technology will shortly provide the brain map that lays out the organization of our brain's multiplicity.

This suggests that it's also important to think beyond multiplicity in intelligence. Most bodybrain systems are multiple. We obviously have multiple sensory/motor systems, and we now know that we have multiple emotional and attentional systems. We've known for some time that we have multiple memory and problem-solving systems. What we have is a multiple-everything bodybrain, and intelligence is only one part of the quite intricate equation. Chapter 4 will further explore this concept.

Thinking about a social brain sparks thoughts of the analogous social organization and management of a classroom—some 30 separate but highly integrated student systems who function separately, in parallel operations, and in competitive and collaborative modes. Collaboratively combining their capabilities generally leads to a better solution of an intriguing problem than the sum of individual solutions—so a class is sort of a social brain.

Dynamic Intelligence

We're used to thinking of intelligence as something that occurs entirely within our brain, but this is now seen as a very narrow view of a complex process that also involves our body and the environment in which our bodybrain functions. *Dynamic* is a better term, one that combines the interactions of the three (Clark, 1998).

Candace Pert, who achieved scientific fame with her endorphin-related discoveries a quarter of a century ago, suggests in *The Molecules of Emotion* (1997) that biology no longer supports the notion of a body-brain separation. Hormonal peptides course throughout our bodybrain to process the emotions that drive our behavior. We are not centered in our brain but in our completely combined body-brain. Consider the negative effects of an upset stomach on test taking if you think that intelligent behavior is all in our head.

Furthermore, we actually tend to off-load a lot of our decision making—creating external procedures and technologies that adjust energy, time, space, and movement in our environmental range to simplify intelligent decisions. For example, consider how much cognitive energy we typically spend in trying to determine which supermarket checkout stand will move the fastest, as compared to the lack of any such thought in a post office or bank with a next-available clerk system. Imagine if a teacher had to decide how to do it every time the class went to the library or cafeteria. Established procedures and rules are integral to classroom life.

Consider the shape of a pair of scissors—how we've created a marvelous technological extension of our hand-finger system that allows us to easily carry out a precise cutting function that would be impossible to do with our fingernails.

We use icons to simplify decisions in complex environments, an extension of the natural clues our ancestors followed to locate water and food. When driving along a succession of gaudy strip malls, easily visible corporate icons help us to decide when and where to turn off for gas, food, lodging, and so forth (and to ignore all other icons that contain information we don't currently need).

Calculators and Post-it™ notes extend our limited short-term memory capacity, and telephone books and dictionaries save long-term memory energy. The list goes on and on. We've created technological capabilities on the outside of our skull to extend our inside biological capabilities, and so we can't measure internal intelligence without factoring in the effects of the external technologies we use. Consider the foot-dragging that occurred in allowing students to use calculators in math tests—as if doing it with paper and pencil was somehow more intellectual (and did ancient educators similarly decry the intellectual loss of finger counting when paper and pencils arrived?).

The recent explosion in electronic and computer technology has moved our dynamic brain-body-environment relationship to a new level. *Natural* time, space, and energy have become *cyber* time, space, and energy, and they've escalated our ability to rapidly organize and process vast amounts of information. One dilemma is that children tend to have a better understanding of the new electronic technologies than their parents and teachers. They've spent countless hours playing with them to explore all their possibilities, while we adults tend to master them only as limited tools—as an expensive typewriter, a means of keeping accounts.

Today's parents and teachers are thus often at a disadvantage when trying to help their children understand the opportunities and dangers that electronic media pose. Our 18 grandchildren are all connected by e-mail, which is a marvelous opportunity, but this capability also means that they can individually engage in chatline conversations with dangerous unseen predators.

The school must confront the dynamic nature and processes of technology, especially electronic technology, but we seem to be moving very slowly. We're the last pencil-driven institution in our society.

I've long felt that the slow movement of multiple computers into the classroom was more related to classroom management than to finances. Educators couldn't figure out what to do with a big box-like monitor on each student desk (let alone electrical cords everywhere). Teachers are used to seeing the top half of their students' bodies out in the open and not hiding behind monitors. The emergence of relatively inexpensive, powerful, portable, networked laptop computers that resemble an unobtrusive three-ring notebook binder on top of a desk suggest that a computer at every desk (with all its attendant management problems) is something that could occur relatively soon.

(Humans seem to enjoy savanna environments—low grassy vegetation with a scattering of trees, as in parks and suburban yards. In some ways, a traditional classroom resembles a savanna—the complex of desktops being the low vegetation and the students a scattering of trees.)

Distributed Intelligence

Our upright stance and consequent necessarily narrow female birth canal have led to a brain that is born only one-third its adult size (as compared to most animals that are born with an almost fully developed brain). The biological solution to the problem is to be born with a full complement of neurons, but with most neural systems functioning at only a survival level. These protosystems then mature by expanding their connections as environmental challenges dictate (and this explains the nature of the postbirth size increase). Thus an infant can innately suckle and cry but must later learn to use its mouth and voice to sing songs. The startle reflex (fear) is innate, but the child must explicitly learn how to cross a busy intersection.

We need a long childhood and explicit instruction to expand the power of our complex of neural protosystems so they can function at the sophisticated level our culture requires. This requires some kind of extended bonding between parents and between parents and child (and oxytocin, vassopressin, and endorphin seem to play important neurochemical roles in this process). Add kinship extensions, and children grow up in a dependent society. Someone will care for them during their first two decades, but then the social contract is that they will spend the next several decades caring for their children (and the children of others in our complex taxed society).

So we are of necessity a social species. This innate sense of dependence means that everyone in a social group must be able to do some communal things (such as being able to speak the common language), but not everyone has to be able to do everything (such as being able to repair a car). Repairing a car requires specialized knowledge and skills that require extensive training, but we don't often need to repair our car. Thus, it's to everyone's advantage for a few people to specialize in car repair and maintain their abilities by doing it as a vocation while others specialize in something else. It's a complex tit-for-tat negotiating arrangement (you repair my car, and I'll teach your children) and an extension of the concept of a dynamic brain that provides our species with an additional powerful social brain. And it's simply another reason to encourage school activities that develop collaborative skills and attitudes.

School assessment programs have focused on individual student capabilities and limitations—and it's good to help students discover how their interests and abilities can be channeled into an appropriate useful vocational specialization. The seeming need for precision in assessment led to a focus on factual and computational knowledge that can be easily and precisely assessed at the cost of ignoring subjective knowledge (as in the arts and humanities), which is more difficult to precisely assess. So I look in vain for reports on the arts and humanities scores when the newspapers report the results of local school testing programs. Are 26 letters and 10 digits and name/date/place information all that our brain is about?

Daniel Goleman's (1995) excellent synthesis of the dramatic advances in emotion research alerted many educators to the terrible error we've made—to use assessment precision as a principal criterion for determining curricular importance. We've ignored the important role that emotionally driven subjective thought and curricula play in intellect. Is it really possible to remove the arts and humanities as a factor in developing intelligence?

The marvelous thing about our integrated bodybrain (our modular/gradient plastic brain and its dynamic distributed intellect) is that its definitive properties include a wide array of capabilities that emerged over eons to respond successfully to dangers and opportunities but also to create a qualitative social life that involves loyalties, the arts, science and the humanities, belief systems, and the ability to enjoy a beautiful sunset. We do disservice to our bodybrain when we provide it with limited opportunities during its formative years. If our students can do something, they ought to have an opportunity to learn to do it properly and effectively. That's the challenge our profession confronts as we now discover our bodybrain as we never could before.

CELLS AND CLASSROOMS

Life is an elusive concept—except that it exists in time and space and requires energy. The current continuing cultural controversy over abortion and euthanasia suggests that we have trouble identifying life's timing—its beginning and ending. But we also have trouble locating it in space. Is life a property of the entire organism, or does it reside within individual organs, tissues, cells, or complex molecules such as DNA? We have further problems with its energy source. Is life's energy nothing more than the activity of self-organizing biological systems, or does it involve such disembodied concepts as mind, spirit, soul, or god? Is life something that exists or doesn't, like an on/off switch, or is it emergent, like a dimming switch (and if so, what's its range)?

Three properties that are common (at several different levels) to all living organisms are (1) a semipermeable membrane covering,

(2) a storehouse of unorganized nutrient materials, and (3) an organizing agent. Whether this combination of properties is actually the essence of life is an issue beyond this discussion, but these properties are important to living organisms, so let's muse about them within the context of the management of a cell and a body and a classroom.

In this metaphoric exploration, and in those to follow, I may muse on well after you've made the connection or stretch the metaphor beyond what you would prefer. Please indulge me in this since I'm trying to provide a broad metaphoric base that teachers can use with a variety of students.

Semipermeable Membrane

A cell and a body exist in space, and so their covering defines their location. In cells, the covering is called a semipermeable membrane, and in a human bodybrain, it's the 6-pound, 20–square foot, two-layer mantle of skin that covers our body to keep our insides in place, heat in, and infection out.

Cells and bodies interact with their outside environment, so they need mechanisms that know what to admit and exclude and that can process the in-and-out movement of materials. In a cell, these processes are carried out by receptors on the membrane that recognize various materials and channels through the membrane that processes their in/out movement. In our body, our sensory system recognizes friends and foes, and our 30-foot long digestive tube and genital system are the principal conduits for the in/out movement of organic materials. But what about the recognition of such things as love and hate and the in/out movement of energy to process and express them? Does behavior become the avenue for sending out such messages that seem to transcend mere organic material?

The semipermeable membrane is thus an important concept in biological systems because it's about what to let in and what to exclude. So it's about food and drink, beautiful music, rape, the smell of flowers, cigarette smoke, conversation, profane and obscene comments, and a whole lot of other things. It's also about the internal products that leave our body, such as urine, semen, babies, and nursing milk but also poems, condolences, inventions, and imaginative lessons.

A classroom also has a semipermeable membrane around it. The walls, ceiling, and floor provide the basic separation from the rest of the community, and the doors, windows, electrical outlets, and faucets allow the in/out flow of students and information. They bring in televised messages from distant places and speakers from the neighborhood, children from functional and dysfunctional families, library books, and show-and-tell artifacts. By extension, a semipermeable membrane is also about a school's admission policies, classroom rules, drug policies, dress code, and hiring practices. At its core, much of classroom management is really about the concept of a semipermeable membrane. Chapter 7 will explore this concept.

Unorganized Nutrient Material

The constant availability of food is a problematic issue for living organisms, so when it's available they must take in and store more than they immediately need. In a cell, this is the nutrient part of the cytoplasm that is immediately available for the assembly of such cellular products as proteins, whenever the need arises. In our body, it includes the fat layers and nutrients that circulate in our bloodstream before they are taken up by cells. In our brain, it includes basic memory units and problem-solving strategies that we can combine to solve novel problems when we confront them.

Think conceptually of the difference between potential and kinetic energy. Potential energy is the stored energy available in a stationary rock poised at the top of a hill, and kinetic energy is what's expressed when the rock rolls down the hill.

Much of our body's weight is composed of currently unused fluids that slosh around, waiting to get organized into something that becomes a body part or behavioral (kinetic) energy. Stored things that aren't currently in use are thus important to biological survival—and we typically have a lot of potential energy within us. How much should be stored can become a biological issue, however, whether it's excess fat on our body, excess sugar or salt stored within our system, or excess drugs taken into our brain. The same can also be said about the excess arcane curricular information that took a lot of energy to get into our brain but has a very limited chance of ever turning into useful cognitive kinetic energy.

One can cynically think of a classroom as a collection of the unwashed and illiterate, milling aimlessly about while waiting for its

Representative of Adult Civilization to organize things—and if the truth be known, students do spend a lot of time waiting for something significant to occur in classrooms in which the teacher makes all the decisions. Students wait to use classroom equipment, to get their teacher's help or assurance that work is correct, to answer the teacher's question, and to leave the room. The sixth graders in a study conducted by Lyons (1977) averaged the initiation of a waiting period every 8 minutes, and generally they were waiting for their teacher's attention.

All shelved curriculum and library materials are potential energy, awaiting a kinetic opportunity to move from the shelf into a student's mind. Athletes on the sidelines are potential energy—desperately hoping to get kinetic. Potential and kinetic energy thus are important classroom management concepts, and Chapter 4 will further discuss them.

Organizing Agent

Cells and organisms need a simple efficient agent to organize their nutrient materials into the products and processes that help to define life. In a cell, DNA (deoxyribonucleic acid) in the nucleus and RNA (ribonucleic acid) carry out that function. Think of a cell as a kitchen, DNA as the genetic cookbook that contains recipes for all the proteins that a body can make, and RNA as the cook who reads the DNA recipe for a protein and then assembles it from the materials within the cellular cytoplasm. And just as a cook doesn't generally use all the recipes in a cookbook, so each cell assembles only a very limited number of proteins from the vast repertoire in our body's DNA.

All proteins are made from 20 different amino acids that can be arranged in countless sequences and lengths, just as all 500,000 English words are made from only 26 different letters that can be arranged in a great variety of sequences and lengths. The information in both proteins and words is not coded into the amino acids and letters themselves but rather into the sequence of amino acids and letters and the length of the chain (e.g., go, god, dog, good, goods, etc.). Consider also the infinite number of melodies constructed from sequences of 12 tones and our immense number system constructed from sequences of only 10 digits.

At the body level, our brain has the assignment of initially receiving meaningless sensory information and organizing it into an integrated coherent model of what's occurring outside our body's semipermeable membrane and then responding appropriately. Our brain also uses a functionally simple system—several dozen different kinds of neurotransmitters that move between synaptically connected neurons that function through only two response modes (excitatory and inhibitory).

But something appears to have been added at this level of organization and direction. Cellular protein production is directed by DNA-RNA-cytoplasm interactions, but their simple chemical transformations don't appear to have anything approaching the conscious, purposeful cognitive activity that we sense in directing many of the activities in our brain. New elements are seemingly added as simple systems become more complex.

When we metaphorically move to the classroom level, we tend to think of the teacher, the administration, or the curriculum as being the organizing agent. And like the organizing agents in our cells and bodies, the classroom organizing agent functions through a relatively simple sequential production system—a selection of activities, a schedule that sequences them, a determination of importance that decides how long activities will last (from a short discrete lesson to an extended integrated instructional unit), and a grouping system that ranges from individual students to various groups of students. Chapters 5 and 6 will further discuss this issue.

A semipermeable membrane, an extensive collection of potentially but currently unorganized materials, and an organizing agent—throughout history, this has been a good organizational plan for biological systems at all levels, and that includes classrooms.

Our brain is functionally similar to an interactive collaborating social system.

CHAPTER THREE

The Marvelous Interdependent Bodybrain That Schools Seek to Manage

Chapter 2 introduced the important concept of biological *modularity*—that specific bodybrain systems are dedicated to specific tasks. For example, feet walk and ears capture sounds. But many important biological tasks require complex, widely distributed systems that broadly disseminate materials and/or information. For example, our circulatory system's heart pumps a large assortment of life-sustaining molecules and blood cells through an encompassing artery/vein/capillary system that is supported by various maintenance organs (such as kidneys and lungs). So to simplify a complex process, the veins input blood, the heart pumps it, and the arteries output it.

At the other end of the size scale, we discover that each of our 100 billion neurons is similarly an input/process/output system. A neuron's many dendrite extensions (from the cell body) receive molecular information from other neurons, the cell body processes the information, and the cell body's (typically) single axon extension sends the neuron's molecular response on to other neurons.

Functionally, it sort of resembles a school system, with student admissions *input*, organizational/curricular/instructional/management *processes*, and graduation *output*—and a variety of central office and building subsystems to support and maintain functions.

Those who would collaboratively manage a classroom full of behaving and misbehaving inhabitants must begin, then, with at least a functional understanding of the key biological systems and subsystems that regulate the behavior of each individual and of the entire class group. This chapter will thus describe our principal biological systems and subsystems with a nontechnical focus on functions, so that you can easily use the information to help your students understand parallels between the management of a bodybrain and a classroom. Subsequent chapters will explore how we can use such biological principles and systems to enhance collaborative classroom management policies and practices.

THE PRINCIPAL BRAIN SYSTEMS

Chapter 2 indicated that our brain's 100 billion neurons are organized into hundreds of millions of subcortical nuclei and cortical columns, which are further combined into more than 100 larger integrated processing systems—with many currently ill understood. Let's first examine our brain's bottom/top, back/front, and right/left anatomical organization (schematically illustrated in Figure 3.1 and discussed below) and then its functional organization.

Anatomical Organization

Bottom-to-Top Organization

To expand on Chapter 2, our brain is composed of (1) subcortical structures in and around the (finger-size) brainstem that unconsciously and reflexively regulate such body systems as respiration and circulation and that synthesize and distribute many of the neurotransmitter molecules that move chemical information within and between neural networks, (2) a cerebellum (located behind the brainstem) that coordinates fine movement sequences with sensory information and participates with the frontal lobes in complex planning activities, and (3) a large overlying, six-layer, deeply folded sheet of cortex that consciously and reflectively processes learned information and behaviors. A stack of six 12 × 18 inch sheets of construction paper approximates the thickness and area of the cortex (85% of the mass of our brain).

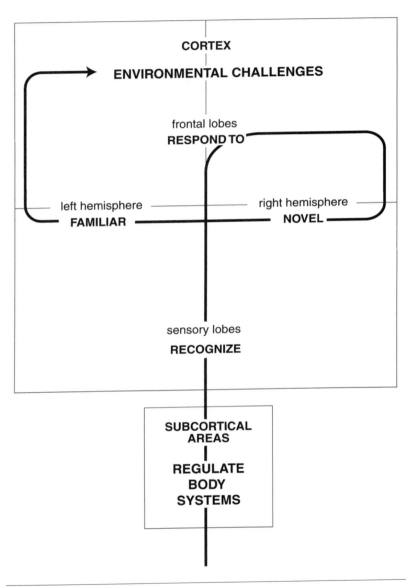

Figure 3.1   Schematic Organization of the Human Brain

Since our immediate environment is rich in dangers and opportunities that range widely in importance, our brain's (principally subcortical) emotional arousal system determines when a specific challenge reaches the threshold of being sufficiently important to activate the several (principally cortical) systems that consciously focus attention and develop appropriate responses. Much of what occurs in teaching and learning is thus focused on activity within the cortex.

Back-to-Front Organization

Simple animal brains unconsciously coordinate recognition information in the thalamus and innate response behaviors in the basal ganglia. More complex animal brains supplement these basic subcortical structures with typically conscious processing systems located in the overlying sheet of cortex:

Recognition: Sensory input and the perceptual integration of that information are processed in the occipital (vision), temporal (hearing), and parietal (touch) lobes, but each lobe also carries out other functions.

Response: Decision-making and behavioral responses are processed in the frontal lobes (30% of the cortex).

Imagine a line across your skull from ear to ear. The sensory lobes of the cortex are principally located in the back (above the thalamus), and the frontal lobes are in the front (above the basal ganglia). So the cortical and subcortical back-to-front organizing principle is that the brain's back section recognizes and creates mental models of dangers and opportunities, and the front section manipulates and transforms these models into a response.

The large human frontal lobes (and especially the prefrontal areas behind our forehead) give us a distinct advantage in recognition and response because they allow us to move from the purely reactive behavior of most animals to being principally proactive—capable of consciously anticipating and preparing for potential novel and familiar challenges.

The prefrontal areas are our brain's functional equivalent of a corporate CEO or symphony conductor who coordinates and integrates the activities of many individuals. Goldberg (2001) reported that the prefrontal cortex is directly interconnected to every distinct functional unit of our brain, and so it coordinates and integrates most brain functions. And like a good computer search engine, it can quickly locate information necessary to decision making.

The importance of effective frontal lobes is further underscored by the growing awareness that many mental disorders (from attention deficits to schizophrenia) are associated principally with frontal lobe malfunction (Andreasen, 2001).

Right-to-Left Organization

Almost all of our brain's recognition and response processing structures are also divided into connected right and left units.

Goldberg (2001) suggested that the fundamental organizing principle for the right and left units emerges out of an important question a brain must ask whenever danger or opportunity looms: Have I confronted this challenge before? He provides considerable research evidence to argue that the right hemisphere (in most humans) is organized principally to process novel challenges, and the left hemisphere processes familiar routines. For example, we process strange faces principally in our right hemisphere and familiar faces in the left. Musically naive people process music principally in their right hemisphere, trained musicians in the left.

Goldberg (2001) argued that although both hemispheres are active in processing most cognitive functions, the relative level of involvement shifts from the right to the left hemisphere over time and with increased competence. The right hemisphere is thus organized to rapidly and creatively respond to a novel challenge (even if it isn't the best solution), but the more linear organization of the left hemisphere eventually translates the initial responses into a more efficient established routine that is activated whenever the challenge reoccurs. Think of the right hemisphere as a company's New Products Division and the left hemisphere as the Production Division.

This division makes sense. Grammatical language is an efficient established procedure to enhance communication within a socially complex species, so it's not surprising that considerable left-hemisphere space is devoted to it. A dependent infant uses whatever (principally right-hemisphere) nonverbal communication skills it can creatively muster to get the help it needs but happily spends much of its childhood mastering the much more efficient existing cultural language template that we pass from generation to generation.

Similarly, children don't have to create personal routines for many other cognitive functions—from tying shoes to flying kites. We teach them how to do it. There's no inherent logic to the order of the letters of the alphabet, but it makes sense (for data classification purposes) for everyone to use the same sequence, so preschool children learn the alphabet song long before they need to use a dictionary.

Functional Organization

If we *functionally* examine our bottom/top, back/front, and right/left brain and its processes, we discover that it has specific complex systems (with processing elements located in many brain areas) that become aware of and respond to internal and external challenges (input/process/output), and the process generally follows a rapid logical biological sequence—a sequence with intriguing parallels to the typical design and management of classroom instruction.

Important internal and external sensory information activates our arousal/alerting system (emotion), which activates our focusing system (attention), which activates our various solution systems (learning/memory, reason/logic, problem solving), which activate our response systems (behavior, movement). We thus cognitively engage, solve, and act (input/process/output). Each of these three major functions is processed by specific dedicated brain systems and subsystems—our multiple-everything brain.

As suggested earlier, our brain is awesomely complex biologically but elegantly simple functionally. Since even primary grade students can understand its functional components, what follows is useful background information you can use to introduce your students to our brain and its functions—with a goal to help them understand the underlying biology of collaboration.

Engage

All cognitive activity is dependent on the initial activation of our integrated sensory/emotional/attentional system. It's biologically impossible to learn something if we're not attending to it, and we don't attend to things that aren't emotionally meaningful to us. Educators have always intuitively known this—and yet some teachers continue to speed through this key initial process with a single dreary directive (e.g., "Clear your desk, take out your math book, and work the problems on page 23").

Since the brain sciences are now discovering how this important integrated activation system functions, we should seek to understand and emphasize it (and Chapter 4 further explores the management implications of this concept). Truly engaged students will actually do much of their exploring and learning during nonschool time, thus expanding the curriculum. We see this in childhood hobbies. Emotionally engaged children spend countless attentive hours of independent reflective time pursuing their new interest.

Senses. Our sensory system is our initial source of information on what's happening inside and outside our body's 20–square foot mantle of skin. It's composed of a complex set of specialized receptors imbedded in our skin that monitor relatively narrow ranges of properties of the internal and surrounding environment. They respond especially to high-contrast changes in the composition and movement of molecules and light rays that strike our body (such as changes in temperature, air and physical pressure, reflected light rays, and the chemical composition of air, water, and food). The human visual and auditory systems are dominant, but all systems play key initial roles in our brain's task of creating perceptual meaning out of abstract sensory information.

Recent educational thought has strongly and appropriately encouraged educators to emphasize activities that engage and develop all elements of our sensory system.

Emotion. *Emotion* is a general term for a complex, critically important, three-part arousal system that unconsciously interprets and evaluates sensory information, thus alerting us to current and potential dangers and opportunities that reach our emotional threshold. It must alert us when we're asleep or attending to other things but not bother us with problems and processes that don't require conscious attention. For example, emotion alerts us to an opportunity for food, but it doesn't continually report on the digestive process that follows eating unless the food turns out to be indigestible.

Furthermore, we don't consciously choose to become emotionally aroused, and such arousal often interferes with what we're currently doing. In effect, our emotions tell us to stop doing what we're doing and to attend to this more important challenge. That dominance is possible because far more neural fibers project from our brain's emotional centers into the logical and rational centers than the reverse. A sudden emotional stimulus can thus easily and immediately stop classroom activity—and it's then neurologically difficult to get folks to rationally shut off their emotional arousal and resume what they were doing. It's best to realize that the disruptive emotional arousal will continue until the problem is resolved and to simply take the time to resolve it before resuming the previous activity.

This emotional dominance is especially true of the immature since adults direct much of the decision making and behavior of children. It's thus biologically important that children first develop an efficient emotional system that will alert them to danger and later a solution system that will effectively respond to the challenge.

Emotion tends to respond most vigorously to high-contrast information and to merely monitor or ignore steady states and subtle changes. This is generally biologically sensible. Stay the course rather than expend cognitive energy on things that aren't currently problematic and fluctuating. Emotion can thus trick us into not recognizing a gradually encroaching problem until it suddenly becomes menacing. We'll return to this issue during the explanation of our attention system.

Emotional arousal doesn't define or solve the challenge but rather activates attentional and problem-solving processes that develop the response. We thus don't emotionally respond to a challenge, but rather our emotions alert us to its existence—a subtle but important distinction. So although our emotions play a necessary initial role in the shaping and eventual solution of a problem, they're not a problem-solving system. They may, however, continue to arouse us throughout the attentional/response sequence because it's generally important to maintain interest in the challenge.

Consider an emotionally arousing game (such as a classroom spelling relay) that has no relationship to the skill being taught. The game artificially hypes student emotion in an activity that probably wouldn't of itself arouse enough interest to enhance learning. So even artificial emotion can activate attention, which activates the cognitive systems that memorize the spelling words. Ideally, though, a teacher's emotional trigger to a student activity should be related to the nature of the activity since this will provide a more easily remembered emotional context for the future use of the learned material or behavior. We'll return to this issue in the discussion of learning.

Help your students to understand emotion by comparing it to a biological thermostat set at a specific temperature. If the temperature suddenly drops below that threshold, the thermostat responds by sending a message to the furnace to send more heat. It doesn't *know* that an open door caused the drop in temperature. A thermostat is thus not an astute problem-solving system—closing the door being a much better solution to the problem. Thermostats and emotion are simply technological and biological arousal systems, but it's important for your students to understand that arousal (awareness of the problem) is the first step to the intelligent solution of a problem—so everything begins with emotion.

Temperament and mood can strongly affect our emotional arousal. *Temperament* provides us with a (perhaps innate) lifelong initial emotional response bias to environmental challenges. A person's temperament typically centers somewhere along a continuum between bold/uninhibited and anxious/inhibited (Kagan, 1994), with boldness processed principally in the left hemisphere and anxiousness in the right hemisphere (Siegal, 1999).

Temperament is a useful human trait in that it allows us to take the first step in response quickly and confidently. The bold tend to go forward in curiosity (sensing an opportunity); the anxious tend to go backward in hesitant concern (sensing danger). Since we frequently follow our developing temperamental bias, we tend to become quite competent with it over time. For example, bold people tend to become skilled at responding boldly (similar to handedness, which develops exceptional competence with the favored hand).

It's important for students to realize that it's OK to generally operate out of either end of the temperament continuum. Our society profits from the strengths of those who are typically either cautious or bold (such as investors who specialize in either conservative or risky investments). Indeed, opposite temperaments often marry each other, and the relationship generally profits from the strengths of each (if they both respect their partner's temperament) since life confronts us with both dangers and opportunities. School groups often exhibit a similar temperament range—from staff and students who are stimulated by any novel idea to those who feel threatened by any change.

One classroom problem, however, is that bold and uninhibited students tend to dominate classroom life (while the anxious raise their hand and wait their turn). Anxious and inhibited students may thus develop a sense of inferiority by incorrectly equating boldness with success. The aphorism "Fools rush in where angels fear to tread" speaks to the value of caution—but anxious and inhibited students wistfully note the attention that the bold and uninhibited tend to get.

So it's important that we create a classroom atmosphere that encourages students (and especially those at the anxious and inhibited end of the continuum) to understand and accept themselves for who they are and to positively develop their temperamental bias—but also to explore opportunities to widen their temperamental response range in appropriate situations. For example, cooperative group activities in a collaborative management model help students at both ends of the continuum to discover that the entire group can profit from temperamental diversity, and participants can assume group roles that challenge their temperamental bias.

Mood provides us with a somewhat diffuse but useful short-term (hours to days) emotional response bias that we layer on to our temperament. Mood shifts probably emerge out of fluctuations in the various chemical rhythms and cycles that regulate bodybrain energy levels and functions. Mood thus informs us of our current and perhaps unconscious level of interest in the challenge and of the amount of response energy that we currently have. We may ignore behaviors on one day that would anger us on another. Our fluctuating level of wakefulness and hunger can similarly affect our desire and ability to respond.

It's important that we communicate our current mood to others since they may then temper the demands that they make on us, effectively enhancing our ability to respond appropriately to current dangers and opportunities. And we actually do effectively communicate mood through several poorly understood forms of body language. For example, a friend suggests, "I can see the anger in your eyes." Although one would be hard-pressed to state how a set of eyes can communicate such different moods as anger, joy, despair, and excitement, they seem to do it. We do tend to sense the moods of others and adapt to them if possible.

Students come to school with a wide range of moods. Since mood significantly determines response, consider beginning the day with interactive activities that provide a sense of how the various moods of students might affect their behavior—and then adapt instruction to student moods wherever possible. Teachers commonly use a variety of techniques (such as holiday decorations and activities) to stimulate similar moods in students and so simplify classroom management and instruction.

Realize also that students quickly check out and respond to their teacher's mood. I've discovered that students will tend to be compassionate to a suffering teacher they like but are often quite cruel to a suffering teacher they dislike. It's called tit-for-tat.

Emotion itself (as we typically view it) is the most immediate, direct, and volatile of the three systems that regulate arousal. Layered on to temperament and mood, it's regulated by a collection of unconscious neuronal systems that continually provide a variety of immediate, often high-energy, positive-to-negative response biases to various challenges. We often publicly communicate the nature of our emotional state through mood-enhanced body language (such as with smiles or tears). When emotion reaches our level of consciousness, it becomes a *feeling*—a much more private experience in that no one can truly *know* how we feel, even though we may talk about it. The conscious state of a *feeling* is what activates a conscious search for a solution to the challenge.

Until recently, it was very difficult to study the specific bodybrain systems that regulate emotion, but the field is now rapidly expanding, and we can expect further developments and a better understanding. It's currently not clear how to classify our various emotions (just as it's been difficult to classify the kinds of intelligence).

One way to classify emotions would be to group them temporally and topically—those that respond to events that have already occurred (such as surprise, the acceptance-disgust-anger continuum, and the joy-sadness continuum) and those that prepare us to respond to events that are about to occur (such as anticipation and fear). Furthermore, the simultaneous activation of two or more of these primary emotions results in a blended emotion (such as surprise + fear = alarm, or anticipation + fear = anxiety—often a dysfunctional blended emotion since it focuses our emotional system entirely on what might occur while ignoring what is occurring). Some emotional states (such as guilt, embarrassment, pride, and jealousy) seem triggered by social events. Researchers currently best understand the neural systems that process fear and joy (or pleasure).

It's important to realize that emotions (like temperament) are neither positive nor negative in themselves. The mechanisms for each emotion evolved to bias and increase the vigor of our response to a specific type of immediate problem. The point is to avoid having such a low firing threshold for one emotion (such as fear) that it dominates all emotional responses or to activate an inappropriate emotion (something that occurs when people cry during weddings and laugh during funerals). Developing emotional competence is thus important in all educative activities.

Goleman's (1995) *Emotional Intelligence* introduced many educators to the important role that emotion plays in cognition. Goleman and now others argue persuasively that educational activities can enhance the development and maintenance of our overall emotional system (defined here as encompassing temperament, mood, and emotion) so that it alerts us appropriately to dangers and opportunities. Young people need to create a functional balance between unconscious emotional arousal and conscious rational response that capitalizes on the role of each. Studies of people who have created such a positive balance in their lives have led to the identification of the several elements discussed below that are critical to the personal/people skills that lead to the intelligent use of emotion, and so it's important to incorporate them into classroom life.

- *Intrinsic Motivation.* Intrinsic motivation is the self-starter's ability to persist in frustrating situations. This ability emerges out of an environment that encourages the discovery and exploration of personal interests and abilities. Such experiences create our self-concept (how we define ourselves) and our level of self-esteem (how we value that definition). Continuous informal evaluations that focus more on what we *can do* than on what we *didn't do* create a necessary climate of positive social feedback. Helpful activities are those that value and discuss feelings, encourage multiple and cooperative approaches to problem solving, and encourage self-assessment.

- *Impulse Control.* Impulse control is the ability to delay decision and gratification. Regrets and apologies are a part of human life—and prisons are full of people who wish that they had counted to 10 before acting. Our wary emotional brain often reads *immediacy* into situations that don't require immediate arousal and response and that are better solved through delayed reflective thought. Developing a pattern of assertive (rather than aggressive) response to difficult situations enhances impulse control. Helpful activities are those that develop problem-solving skills and focus on long-term projects with intermediate goals (so participants can experience and appreciate things that develop slowly).

• *Mood Regulation.* Mood regulation involves the ability to regulate moods (and especially those related to anger) so that distress doesn't reduce our ability to think and reflect. There's a fine line between simply experiencing mood for what it is and allowing it to dominate our entire behavior. Although we may occasionally (and perhaps unfortunately) step over that fine line, it's probably worse to be so controlled emotionally as to never step over it. Helpful activities are those that teach students to understand and respect emotional arousal without necessarily submitting to it and that provide a forum for venting positive and negative emotion, as well as an opportunity to retreat from social interaction when emotion overwhelms.

• *Empathy.* Empathy involves the ability to empathize, with a sharing, caring, and hopeful sense of how the other person feels about something. Sympathy differs from empathy in that it's a kind-hearted recognition of the plight of another without the sense of sharing it that empathy implies. Empathy is an important social trait in that it leads to ethical and altruistic behaviors. Helpful activities are those that encourage constant open discussion of how things are going to help students tune into each other (to develop useful listening, looking, and responding skills in conversation).

• *Social Competence.* Social competence involves the ability to quickly size up and appropriately respond to social situations. Our complex social structure functions via our innate sense of cooperation, early experiences with adults and children, and a set of social rules (or manners) that might actually be quite arbitrary and culture driven. Manners thus don't come naturally but must be taught. Helpful activities are those that encourage the constant informal interactions that allow participants to discover how others respond to their behavior and that specifically teach the social conventions a group must observe if they are to effectively work together. Activities such as cooperative learning projects, games, field trips, and reflective discussions do this.

Attention. Emotional arousal is an indication that something important has occurred or is about to occur. But where? To find out, our emotions activate attention, a complex cognitive system that selects and temporarily focuses on key emotionally important elements in an often-confusing environment and maintains goal-directed behavior in highly distractible situations. It thus separates an emotionally significant foreground from the less significant background. The frame on a picture, the zoom lens on a camera, the stage in an auditorium, and cosmetics such as eyeliner and lipstick are all technologies that help to direct attention—to separate foreground from background.

Our attentional system is composed of a number of distinct neural networks, each of which actively carries out specific attentional functions by itself or in interaction with other cognitive systems. Since experience and educational interventions can improve the efficiency of this complex system, we should design school activities that enhance the development of the three separate functional systems that regulate attention.

The *orienting system* disengages us from what we were attending to and focuses us on the new challenge. We generally shift our attention to emotionally arousing things that contrast sharply with our current focus and ignore (or merely monitor) steady states, subtle differences, and gradual changes that don't carry a sense of immediacy. For example, when we leave a building, we consciously notice the temperature when it's much different outside than inside but not when both are similar. We (and especially students) use the term *boring* to describe a steady-state environment with few emotionally stimulating challenges.

Our environment, however, is replete with serious dangers (such as pollution) that are subtle and gradual. They're emotionally significant, but we tend to focus on them only when a high-contrast catastrophe (such as a toxic spill) occurs. The *news* is about the unusual, not the normal, so it reports a single freeway pile-up of 10 cars but not the perhaps 100 individual fender benders that occurred in the same general area that day. Graphs and time-lapse photography are examples of the many technologies we've developed to observe changes that occur too gradually to activate our biological emotion and attention systems. Many children's games (from Simon Says to video games) require participants to identify and attend to important subtle clues, so children do tend to enjoy the challenge of subtlety.

An important element in successful classroom management is the ability to note and orient to subtle changes in students that might lead to behavioral disruptions. During my first year of teaching, I expended much energy on classroom management problems and was generally unsuccessful. Several years later, I spent far less energy on management and had fewer problems. I now realize that much of the difference emerged out of experiences that taught me to attend to potential problems before they became real problems. In effect, I moved from being a few steps behind my class to a couple steps in front of them.

The *executive attention system* draws heavily on memory to recognize the identity of the new challenge (foreground), determine its significance, and separate it from the background information (which it then merely monitors or ignores). This is typically an efficient unconscious process that draws on established responses, but we do confront situations in which it's not obvious what we should focus on in a confusing situation. In such situations, our executive attention system must consciously make the decision—such as to respond to a novel situation that will require planning and decision making, to alter a habitual response, or to correct an error. The broad appeal of magicians and mystery stories suggests that we're stimulated by this conscious element of attention.

Our working (or short-term) memory is an important part of this system. It's a fragile, limited capacity buffer that allows us to briefly attend to and hold a few units of information while we use it (dial the phone number) or determine its importance (the name of a stranger in a party conversation). It's about things that are important right now but not so important that we want to remember them for the rest of our life. The limited capacity of working memory is useful since it forces us to combine related bits of information into larger units by identifying similarities, differences, and patterns that can simplify and consolidate an otherwise large and confusing sensory field. Vocabulary categories emerged out of this cognitive ability.

Students need many opportunities to develop this important system. We should incorporate many options that require participants to make choices that they can later reflect on to determine the wisdom of their choice. Furthermore, working memory is enhanced by activities that require participants to rapidly classify large numbers of items into a smaller number of categories. Discussions and debates similarly require participants to consciously select and attend to limited information for a limited time.

The *vigilance system* has the reverse task of the orienting system. Vigilance maintains a sustained focus on something while ignoring small, random, potentially distracting environmental changes. The vigilance system thus helps us to ignore minor but not major distractions. A major distraction may lead to an emotional arousal that activates our orienting system, and we're off to a new focus of attention. We typically can simultaneously attend to several noncompeting events (such as to look at a person while conversing and arranging chairs around a table) but not competing events (such as to simultaneously carry on a face-to-face and phone conversation).

The pop-out phenomenon is an intriguing element in vigilance. It's the unexpected experience we often have of suddenly recognizing a friend in a large group of people we're merely monitoring. It probably has something to do with unique features our friend has that aren't shared by the surrounding people, but this remarkable attentional property is currently ill understood.

As remarkable as our vigilance system is, it isn't good at sustaining attention on tasks that are oriented to precise details and contain only subtle environmental shifts. Many educational activities require students to maintain vigilant attention (such as while working a page of similar math problems), and teachers often have management problems when they extend such study periods.

Vigilance is an important component in most games children play (from tag to video games), so they seem to have an almost innate sense that they need to develop the system. It's good, therefore, to create activities that enhance students' ability to decide whether to maintain a current attentional focus and then to make intelligent choices about short- and long-term attentional tasks.

Our three-part attention system thus moves us from arousal to focus. It's a sort of zoom lens that can zoom in to identify and carefully examine details (foreground) or zoom out to scan the context (background).

Although educators have been especially concerned about attention-deficit hyperactivity disorder (ADHD), it's important to realize that malfunctions in one or more of the subsystems that regulate attention can lead to many mental illnesses and learning handicaps (such as anxiety, autism, bipolar disorder, dyslexia, hyperactivity, mental retardation, obsessive-compulsive disorder, and schizophrenia). Furthermore, many accidents and much classroom misbehavior involve attentional lapses. Medications and behavioral interventions exist to help those whose deficits in one or more elements of the attentional system are related to chemical imbalances, developmentally weak neuronal pathways, and/or learned inappropriate behavior patterns.

Since attentional malfunctions create such serious human problems, it's becoming evident that attention is a more central cognitive system than many thought it to be. Indeed, emotion and attention may be the integrated cognitive system that is most closely related to consciousness, long the Holy Grail of the cognitive neurosciences.

As indicated above, consciousness involves our subjective awareness of and focus on a small part of the vast amount of information our brain is currently processing, which is pretty much what emotion and attention regulate. Damasio (1999) suggested that consciousness is the relationship of an organism to another organism or object, expressed as a *feeling*. Feelings, which lead us to conscious thought and reflective exploration of the current challenge, are thus useful since they allow us to go beyond innate programmed behaviors to rationally design solutions to a variety of contemporary challenges that evolutionary development didn't cover.

So consciousness is a key factor in our subjective recognition of our irresistible biological urge to stay alive and to develop a concern for our own self and for other selves. Emotion and attention are thus central to collaborative classroom management, and so it's important that teachers explain the systems to their students.

Solve

Solutions to the many internal and external challenges that we confront emerge out of a complex set of interacting conscious and unconscious neuronal systems that involve such cognitive elements as learning and memory, reason and logic, and a wide range of reflective and reflexive problem-solving strategies. Various theories of intelligence (that combine these cognitive elements) have emerged, and these purport to classify the kinds of problems we confront and the general reflective cognitive strategies we use to solve them.

Since Gardner's (1983, 1998) theory of multiple intelligences is perhaps the best known of these theories among educators, I briefly adapted it below to reflect the functional brain systems that regulate it. To simplify the discussion, I'll use Gardner's categories as a focus in subsequent chapters that explore (among other things) the classroom management implications of intelligent and nonintelligent behavior. This practical approach should thus serve as a useful parallel to the extensive current literature on the curricular and instructional applications of Gardner's theory.

But in doing this, I want to underscore that strong biological correlates exist also for other current excellent widely respected theories of intelligence, such as those of Perkins (1995) and Sternberg (1985). Educators interested in the concept of multiple intelligences should explore the entire literature and not just the work of one theorist, and so I would encourage you to read articles and books by Sternberg and Perkins, in addition to those by Gardner.

Reflective Problem-Solving Systems. Some nonthreatening environmental challenges don't require immediate solutions. They focus on life's continuing challenges with our personal/social identity and with natural and electronic space/time. Solutions often emerge slowly, on the basis of a reflective exploration of the factual objective elements of a situation. We can functionally arrange Gardner's (1983, 1998) nine forms of intelligent reflective response into three sets of three basic identity, space, and time problem categories that define human life. The assumption of modularity is that each of these intelligent response systems is processed by dedicated specialized neuronal systems that would be very much interconnected with systems that process the other forms of intelligence.

Intelligence subsystems with an inward focus:

- Who? Personal/Social/Existential Intelligence
  Who am I, and who are these people around me? What does it mean to exist? (Gardner: Intrapersonal/Interpersonal/Existential Intelligences) Chapter 8 (and to an extent Chapter 4) will explore the management implications of these concepts.

Intelligence subsystems with an outward focus:

- Where? Space/Place Intelligence
  Where am I, and how can I get from here to there? How is nature organized? (Gardner: Spatial/Bodily-Kinesthetic/Naturalist Intelligences) Chapter 5 will explore the management implications of these concepts.

- When? Time/Sequence Intelligence

How long has this been going on, what should we do about it, and what will happen if we carry out our plans? (Gardner: Language/Musical/Logical-Mathematical Intelligences) Chapter 6 will explore the management implications of these concepts.

The process of the reflective solution of a problem begins with *the past,* our learning/memory system that searches for information related to previous similar situations. Learning is how our brain acquires new information, and memory is how and where our brain stores it. Learning/memory is a large part of what we manage in classrooms, so we need to understand it if we hope to manage it.

Scientists generally divide memory into several systems: (1) a short-term/limited-capacity system called working memory (discussed above) that has no long-term recall and (2) a more complex long-term memory system that unconsciously processes skills (procedural memory), such as knowing how to touch-type, and that consciously processes factual label-and-location information (declarative memory).

Scientists further subdivide declarative memory into autobiographical memories of personal experiences (episodic memory), such as our memory of learning how to type, and cultural memories of more abstract and symbolic objects, events, and relationships (semantic memory), such as knowing common elements on all word processors. We further tend to remember when and where specific episodic learning activities took place, but not semantic learning. For example, I remember studying spelling in elementary school, but I don't remember when I learned to spell *accommodate* correctly. So our memory mechanisms are complex, and though still ill understood, they form the substrate of all curricula—and factual memory formation and recall tend to dominate classroom activity.

Since emotion is the *thermostat* that activates the attentional focus that may lead to learning/memory, we create separate emotional memories that help to spark the activation (and a subcortical almond-shaped structure called the amygdala appears to play an important role in processing emotional memories). Think of factual memory as being more about remembering *what happened* and emotional memory as being about remembering *how I felt about what happened.* Both are important, but our emotional memories are the more powerful (our emotional memories of childhood, for example, are stronger than our remembrance of all the factual details of childhood).

Factual memory formation and recall require emotional time and space associations with the various elements of a perceived object or event (such as whether a history fact will be on the test). A factual memory is thus tied to its context and so is easily learned and forgotten. If school requirements are the only context for the material to be learned, it's easily forgotten when we leave school—as all of us have experienced as students. Misbehavior often occurs when students are required to learn things that have no context for (or emotional relationship to) their personal lives.

The following memory metaphor explains and so helps us to understand the important relationship between our emotional and factual memories (Sylwester & Margulies, 1998).

When we're overwhelmed by information and/or challenges, we tend to reinvent the related body-brain process outside of our body and let that technology carry the load. Examples include phone books, dictionaries, calculators, and photographs. Thus, in our search for a simple explanation for emotional and factual memory, it's useful to metaphorically explore the systems outside of our skull that we've developed to store and retrieve complex combinations of information.

The combination of file cabinet, file folders, and files might be a useful metaphor for memory—one that you and your students can easily explore since it has many parallels to what our brain actually does as it gathers, organizes, stores, retrieves, and uses information.

Think of your brain as a reasonably full and useful file cabinet. Think then of an emotional memory as a file folder (within a cabinet drawer) that contains many files—the factual memories of specific objects and events related to the emotion. When you pull out a file folder, you have easy access to all the files within it. When the file folder is in the file cabinet, though, you don't have easy access to the files.

It's useful to limit ready access to many of our factual memories to situations in which we're in the time/space/emotional *neighborhood*. Imagine a trip to the downtown area of a city you've visited, but not recently. Before going, you may have trouble recalling specific locations, stores, cafés, and so on, but when you arrive in the area, many factual memories easily return. The emotional state of being there automatically pops out the file folder, and you have ready access to the factual information you need.

Imagine the cognitive overload if we had continuous easy access to all such factual memories even when we didn't need them, when we weren't in the neighborhood. Or think of how we effortlessly recall long-dormant memories of people and events while attending a class reunion or the instant recall of prior related negative experiences during an argument with a spouse or friend.

We thus have the best access to weak factual memories (the files) through strong emotional memories (the file folders). Factual memories without emotional context are difficult to store and retrieve. The names/dates/places kinds of curricular information we ask students to remember are a good example. Students often ask, "Will this be on the test?" and if the answer is yes, they then have a useful *emotional file folder* for the information: test things. During the test, they'll psychologically pull out and use the file folder and its names/dates/places information, but as indicated above, it's quite questionable if the file folder will ever come out in any nontest situation. School simulation and role-playing activities thus provide a useful emotional context (or file folder) because they are related to real-life emotional uses of the information. Conversely, multiple-choice (and related) tests generally mask the context of factual information. The result is that students often associate the facts with the test rather than with their cultural utility. Students who pass the test may still be unable to retrieve and use the information in its cultural context.

If the emotional overtones of an experience are very important, we may create especially strong emotional and weak factual memories of the event. Thus, an abused child who must continue to live in an abusive situation may be better off focusing on aversion strategies than on remembering all the details of past abuse. A strong related emotional stimulus years later may then trigger the recall of these weak factual memories (as also occurs with long-dormant school memories at a class reunion; Kandel & Kandel, 1994).

Mass media, marketers, politicians, and special interest groups often exploit our emotional/factual memory system by hammering us with emotion-laden terms and images that they design to pull out emotional file folders biased to their position. Two such placard-waving groups with opposite views on the issue of Internet censorship regulations recently appeared in the same newspaper picture—one waving a sign with the message "Stop Child Pornography!" and the other "Protect Our First Amendment Rights!" How newspaper readers will contemplate the issue will depend somewhat on which file folder popped up in a reader's mind upon seeing the picture and whether the "facts" supporting the position were seriously biased. Similarly, emotion-laden terms related to such cultural areas as race, ethnicity, gender, religion, and sexual behavior will quickly spark response.

Even if we don't already have an emotional file folder for an issue we confront for the first time, we tend toward an almost immediate emotional response (such as when terrorists used passenger planes as guided missiles to destroy New York City's World Trade Center). Think of the organization of a library. If the book we seek is gone, we usually examine the two adjacent books because libraries are organized so that the two adjacent books are always the closest in focus or content to any shelved book. Similarly, when we confront a novel challenge, our emotional system tends to begin our response sequence with something we consider metaphorically similar. In the case of the World Trade Center bombing, perhaps the concept of religious martyrs or the World War II Japanese kamikaze pilots popped up in your mind.

Reflective solutions thus emerge within the context of our rational analysis of the *present* problem—an analysis that considers *past* related remembered experiences and the possible *future* effects of our decision. Our complex solution systems thus nimbly traverse our human space/time framework—here/there and past/present/future.

A number of programs that purport to teach specific reflective thinking and problem-solving strategies have emerged in recent years, and we can expect more. All report success, and so it may well be that it doesn't make too much difference which approach a program uses as long as it works and complements the focus of the school's curriculum and the comfort level of those who implement it. Student brains tend to resist programs that aren't tuned to their cognitive rhythms.

Issues in memory and problem solving are central to the current politically powerful but biologically naive standards and assessment movement. Many patrons consider it reasonable to require educators to develop a simple one-size-fits-all assessment program that will precisely measure a student's imprecise memory and problem-solving ability.

Goldberg (2001) used the terms *veridical* and *adaptive* knowledge in his analysis of our brain's thinking and decision-making systems—and his analysis explains why it's so difficult to precisely measure knowledge and also why a collaborative classroom management model fits so well into the kinds of thinking processes that students must develop.

Veridical knowledge is knowing the answer to a problem that has a single correct answer: $6 \times 5 = 30$, Salem is the capital of Oregon, c-a-t spells *cat*. It's the product-oriented essence of *true/false*—and it's the quintessential element of such culturally popular activities as crossword puzzles and TV quiz shows (in which the winning contestant has the best command of the least important, most obscure veridical information). In school, students must discover and remember the hidden answers to clear-cut veridical questions they didn't ask (and for which they often have no personal context).

Veridical knowledge is an obviously important cognitive (and school assessment) element, but *true/false* isn't always as clear-cut as many folks think (Gardner, 1999). For example, mastering one's native language is a major juvenile task. The hundreds of thousands of words in our language are veridical in that each represents a clearly defined category. Still, it's much easier to precisely define some concepts (such as *male*) than others (such as *chair*). But even a precisely defined primary concept (*male*) may have many synonyms (such as *man, gentleman, guy, chap, fellow*) that are used interchangeably in common discourse, even though each synonym has a distinct meaning.

Furthermore, English spelling allows for few acceptable variants, but most people could easily read the word *accommodate* when misspelled in several different ways. E-mail has further confounded standard spelling with a growing number of abbreviations (such as *U* for *you*) that folks readily use to speed up electronic discourse. Mark Twain's comment that only an uncreative person can think of but one way to spell a word seems apropos.

Our brain is fortunately sufficiently adaptable so it can function with information that's only fairly close to precise truth. Furthermore, we tend to off-load information that requires memorized precision to such technologies as calculators, telephone books, spell checkers, and dictionaries. And even then, the technological precision that e-mail addresses require frustrates our imprecise brain whenever a message gets rejected because of a single-letter error in the address.

Veridical knowledge is important, but its cultural precision is often overrated, and it's not the principal element of intelligent human behavior.

Adaptive Knowledge and Decisions. Goldberg (2001) called the cognitive processes that lead to a personal preference among alternatives *adaptive* thought and decision making. Knowing the names of the presidential candidates is veridical knowledge. Casting my vote is an adaptive decision. Most human thought, decision making, and collaborative management resolutions are adaptive (or actor centered). How do I interpret the facts? What choice is best for me?

We often use veridical information during the process of making an adaptive decision. For example, we look at a restaurant menu before ordering and note such veridical elements as the cost and composition of items. Cost may be important to price-conscious consumers and ingredients to those who are allergic, but the issue of what we should order has no correct or incorrect answer. It's a personal preference based on many factors, and any order is a legitimate decision.

Even U.S. Supreme Court decisions are adaptive. After examining the veridical facts of the case and the relevant carefully worded laws and precedents, the judges may adaptively differ 5-4 on which position in the case is constitutionally correct.

This veridical-adaptive relationship is similar in arts, humanities, and social skills programs that subjectively integrate veridical information into adaptive decisions. All these cognitively important curricular areas have lost their school significance and funding in an era in which precise assessment controls the curricular agenda.

For example, art is a unique expression that's centered on preference. Thus, if it's possible to precisely evaluate art, it's not art—it's reproducible craft. There's nothing wrong with craft; it's just not art. When a noted pianist was asked to explain the difference between a piano player and a pianist, he responded that anyone can play the correct notes. That response gets to the heart of the issue. Playing the correct notes (a veridical act) is important, but the aesthetics of playing the correct notes with adaptive style and grace is more important.

Consider professional basketball. Veridical information (such as scores, averages, and records) dominates sports reporting. Fans want their team to win, but they're generally equally interested in observing the many adaptive decisions that occur during a game—as players follow set plays or improvise shots, coaches send players in and out of the game, and referees respond to or ignore violations. Perhaps more important, fans want both teams to play with the creative style and grace expected of athletic virtuosos. It will thus be possible to identify the champion with veridical certainty at the end of the NBA playoffs, but something is seriously missing in the enterprise if that's all the long season was about.

So is it also with school assessment programs that focus only on objective *true/false* and ignore subjective *right/wrong, good/bad, beautiful/ugly, fair/unfair, ethical/unethical,* and all the other preference-driven decisions that humans continuously make. An assessment program that is principally focused on veridical knowledge misses the point of what our brain's knowledge and decision-making capabilities evolved to do. Conversely, a collaborative classroom management program celebrates them.

Reflexive Problem-Solving Systems. Threatening or opportunistic challenges often require an immediate nonreflective response (such as what to do about a rapidly approaching car or how to take advantage of a fleeting opportunity). Our brain has a separate stress-driven reflexive system that quickly activates powerful, principally innate, but also learned automatic fight-or-flight response programs when the emotional impetus is basically to quickly attack, flee, or mate.

Reflexive responses tend to occur on the basis of high emotional arousal and focus and on limited superficial information because we don't have time to gather all the facts. When survival is at stake, a rapid (even if it's not the best possible) response is preferable to informed death from delay.

Rapid reflexive responses may thus save our lives, but they can also unfortunately lead to the stereotyping (such as in racism, sexism, and elitism), regrets, and apologies that are unfortunately so common when we make fearful, impulsive, and ill-informed responses. Worse, the neurotransmitter and hormonal discharges associated with fear can strengthen the emotional and weaken the factual memories of an event if the stressful situation is serious and/or chronic. We become fearful of something, but we're often not sure why, so we've learned little from the experience that's consciously useful (because a reflexive response occurs unconsciously and reduces our ability to create factual memories).

Some research evidence suggests that the oversecretion of powerful stress hormones (such as cortisol) that accompanies the chronic activation of our reflexive pathways can physically deteriorate key areas of our factual memory and reflective systems

(Sapolsky, 1999). Since the point of a reflexive response is to respond quickly, it's important for our emotion/attention system to turn up the reflexive pathways and to turn down the reflective pathways that would delay the response. The stress hormones enhance the functioning of reflexive pathways, but they can negatively affect the robustness of chronically turned-down reflective pathways.

So what we have is a very powerful and useful stress-driven reflexive response system that should be activated in situations that require an immediate forceful response, such as the sudden accelerations and rapid braking often necessary in averse traffic conditions. The reflexive system evolved, however, to be used as a temporary rather than continuous response system (continuous acceleration and braking when driving is not advisable). So it's like salt: a little bit of it is biologically useful, but a whole lot is generally harmful.

In this light, school physical aggression is a continuing problem (especially among males). Chronic aggressors often respond reflexively and aggressively to minor confrontations that don't warrant such a response, but the aggressor didn't consider alternatives. We're frustrated by such troubling student behavior and tend to seek single simple explanations—mass media, guns, poor parenting and teaching, chemical imbalances—but behavioral biology is generally more complicated than that.

For example, testosterone has long been a chemical candidate to explain male aggression. It's an important steroid with multiple values. It promotes bone growth and muscle mass, lowers the male voice, and helps to develop sexual characteristics. It also binds to brain areas that influence behavior. Both males and females have testosterone, but males have much more than females.

Male testosterone levels surge between ages 10 to 14 before leveling off, and they fluctuate across the day and year. The folk wisdom thus tagged testosterone as the correlation culprit since male aggression also tends to surge in mid-adolescence. Sapolsky (1998) discovered that it isn't that simple. Although all adolescent males experience this adolescent testosterone elevation, not all adolescent males typically respond aggressively to threat.

Two subcortical brain structures, the amygdala and hypothalamus, play key roles in activating our rapid reflexive and often assertive response to an imminent danger or opportunity. Elevated testosterone levels don't trigger such an aggressive response, but they can turn up the volume of an already triggered reflexive response and so escalate simple anger and assertiveness (which could be used positively in a reflective response) into reflexive physical aggression. So it isn't the testosterone that's the culprit; rather, its considerable energy potential is channeled into a reflexive rather than reflective response.

This certainly underscores the importance of helping students not only to understand and respect the power of their survival-oriented reflexive system but also to develop effective reflective capabilities that can override or compensate for the social problems that reflexive responses often cause. Subsequent chapters will focus on this issue.

Unfortunately, some students live in such an insecure fearful environment that their reflexive system seems to run continuously. A condition called *learned helplessness* can result from such an environment. The child eventually senses no personal control over an unpredictable environment and simply gives up the innate drive to cope.

It's thus important to remember, when developing curricular and behavior policies and practices, that chronically fearful home and school environments can biologically diminish a student's ability to learn and remember. To create a chronically stressful school environment to increase learning is thus biologically both counter-productive and irresponsible.

Act

Solutions lead to behavior, and behavioral responses are principally mediated by three sets of appendages that constitute the motor system that gives us our mobility—our leg, foot, and toe system (for moving); our arm, hand, and finger system (for handling and throwing); and our neck, mouth, and tongue system (for talking and eating).

Mobility is perhaps our most definitive property. The reason we and all animals have a brain and plants don't is because we can move on our own volition and power, and plants can't. You don't need a brain if you're not going anywhere. A tree that would profit from moving to where there's more sunlight and nutrients is out of luck. Mobility's significance to human life suggests that educative experiences must activate the entire motor system so that we don't merely move but do so with style and grace. Virtuoso movement is central to the visual, aural, and movement arts. Classroom movement tends to focus on one pencil-laden appendage assembling letters and digits on a playing field the size of a sheet of typing paper. We can and should certainly improve on that—creating activities that stimulate and develop a wide range of movement skill. Chapter 7 will explore the management implications of this concept.

From Jungle to Classroom in Search of a Model

So how does our modular plastic brain develop (and apportion space to) the large number of neural networks it needs to operate the specific functional systems and subsystems described throughout this chapter? And an obviously related question (at least for this book) is as follows: How do 30 or so people who share a classroom develop the collaborative skills to properly apportion energy, space, time, and movement within appropriate ranges to execute the functions society expects of them?

Biological Replication

Edelman (1992) persuasively argues that the evolutionary natural selection processes that shaped our biological environment and basic human brain over long periods of time also shape the developing neural networks of each individual brain over its lifetime. Edelman sees similarities between the rich evolving ecology of a jungle environment and the gradual development of our brain's neural networks. Plants and animals in a jungle area (and neural networks in a brain) function both competitively and symbiotically in response to environmental challenges. The overall result can be a vibrant healthy community—but one that at any given moment also includes opportunity and danger, triumph and tragedy for individual organisms (or neural networks).

The point for an organism is to survive and reproduce. Survival in nature means to locate an ecological niche suited to one's needs and abilities and then to use available energy to gain and protect needed resources and to adapt to changing conditions. Organisms function for their individual survival, not for the good of the species. Those organisms that best adapt to environmental challenges reproduce the most successfully, which may in fact enhance the health of the species but not by deliberate design. Edelman (1992) argues that these same Darwinian principles determine how individual neural networks develop over time. His theory would argue, for example, that differential human abilities and talents would emerge from the development of abnormally large and robust networks in the brain areas that regulate the person's specialty (such as abnormalities in the motor areas that regulate a talented pianist's finger movements).

Cultural Replication

Some scientists further suggest that the same general Darwinian principles govern the cultural replication and evolution of ideas—that many cultural concepts, such as wheels, language, music, clothing, and schools, persist across cultures but gradually change over time. Dawkins (1989a, 1989b) and Blackmore (1999) call these modifiable persistent units of cultural transmission *memes*—analogous to biological genes. They emerge out of the (seemingly unique) ability of humans to imitate the selected cultural behavior of others. For example, children learn how to drink from a cup by observing and copying parental patterns and to speak their native language by copying the speech patterns they hear. We hear a joke and pass it on; we like a clothing style and copy it.

Electronic communication technologies have recently vastly increased our ability to observe and imitate others—well beyond neighborhood confines. We now inhabit a gossipy worldwide electronic village with several hundred million neighbors. The Internet is the ultimate free-for-all in the explosive world of memes.

Mass media unfortunately often mask context—what occurs anywhere is immediately available everywhere, so normal space/time frameworks become confused in the minds of many. For example, a rare and isolated emotionally charged event somewhere can become a rampant phenomenon in the minds of many who followed its extensive media coverage and commentary.

The positive side of this is that it allows us to empathize with people we've never met in person, such as in the wide outpouring of grief that often occurs after a major tragedy. The negative side is that it also leads to the memetic tendency to replicate here what occurred there—and that did occur with the copycat violence and threats of violence after each of the several American school murders that occurred during the final years of this past century. At another less violent level, it also continuously occurs in schools as mass media–driven fashions (such as in clothing, speech, and behavior) quickly spread across the land.

Similarly, many instructional and classroom management practices persist and evolve over long periods of time. For example, classrooms (almost by definition) have long tended to have a dominant *teacher* presence who apportions resources and directs energy expenditures. Conversely, in a balanced ecological system, no one organ or organism dominates. All elements have opportunities to share in resources, and all make long-term positive contributions (although the prey in an area may not especially appreciate the current contribution of its predators).

We can see an ecological parallel in a balanced modular/gradient plastic brain with its many neural networks that operate the functional systems. They must work cooperatively and competitively to enhance the life of the total organism. Each system contributes something important. Mental illness results from the malfunction of one or more important brain systems.

We can see a similar ecological parallel in a democratic society that distributes governance and resources among its citizens, with elected leaders who are answerable to the electorate. Our schools have a major responsibility to develop democratic knowledge, attitudes, and skills in students that will allow them to participate productively, and so we've seen a move toward more democratic classroom management procedures in recent decades—but we're still faced with a fundamental inconsistency between the perceived needs of adult society for efficient effective *managed* schools and the needs of students for a laboratory to explore democratic collaborative policies and practices.

When we begin to think biologically and ecologically, we discover that the classroom management arena provides an excellent laboratory setting for such democratic activity and beyond. Current classroom behavior and misbehavior can actually become important elements of the curriculum. An imaginative class can explore parallels between a playground skirmish and a national war, between class and community collaborative projects. And in the process, they will also discover parallels between life in a classroom and life in an ecological area, such as a jungle or prairie.

As indicated in Chapter 1, this isn't a new or revolutionary idea. It's a tenet of existing democratic classroom management programs.

What such mental exploration does is to begin the process of connecting elements of biology and classroom management. Such thinking leads to the realization that key concepts in biology and ecology aren't any more arcane than day-to-day life in a classroom. They're fundamental, grounded in common sense. Modular plastic brains in a modular adaptable classroom. How exciting!

CHAPTER FOUR

Collaboratively Expending Energy

Who's in Charge?

Energy is the elusive concept that drives all life. When we expend energy in the limited space/time world that we inhabit, movement generally occurs. Energy, space, time, and limited movement are thus key elements of human life—and so they are also key elements in classroom management. Classrooms and their occupants are about *space*, the school year and its schedules and rhythms are about *time,* potential/kinetic *energy* is about behavior (and its antecedents and effects), and behavior causes physical and psychological *movement* within limited biological and cultural *ranges.*

Since everything begins with energy, this chapter will explore the biological and classroom management implications of biological and cultural energy (and the four chapters that follow will focus in turn on space, time, movement, and range). The concept of energy encompasses a mixed bag of subconcepts with important classroom management implications, such as emotion, attention, self-concept/self-esteem, interest, motivation, ability, funding, control, collaboration, rules, and assessment. This chapter will explain biological and cultural energy, define key management issues, and suggest metaphors and activities that could help a class (or staff) to begin the task of devising a collaborative classroom management program that can connect current and potential thought about classroom management to related developments in biology (and especially in the cognitive neurosciences). The subsequent chapters on space, time, movement, and range will provide similarly useful ideas and materials for developing a collaborative classroom management model.

If you are a classroom teacher, consider using the material in this book in the development of an instructional unit for the beginning of the school year. The unit could (1) introduce your students to the energy/space/time/movement/range organization, development, and management of their individual and collective bodybrains and (2) explore how they can best use this understanding of themselves to collaboratively create a comfortably effective classroom environment.

Chapter 2 ended with Edelman's (1992) jungle metaphor related to the development and operation of our bodybrain. It suggests that just as no one organism continually controls a rich ecological environment, so no one biological system continually controls our bodybrain. Rather, our various systems continually shift in their relative levels of importance and in the control they currently exert over other systems.

Institutions are similar. For example, we tend to think of the fire chief as the one who controls the fire department, but it's the person who just turned in an alarm who determines the department's next action—and the student who hit another student (at least momentarily) controls things in the classroom. The issue of who or what controls the classroom (mostly and currently) is thus fundamental to any discussion about the design and implementation of a collaborative classroom management model for the 21st century. It's where to begin, and so what follows is a metaphorical issue that might enhance such an exploration.

CHILDBIRTH, CHILDHOOD, AND CLASSROOMS

Chapter 1 suggested that we could think of the students in a classroom as a collective living social organism. Its metaphoric properties include the semipermeable membranes, unorganized nutrient materials, and organizing agent that characterizes life at various levels. We humans have about a couple dozen organs in our body, and a classroom has about a couple dozen inhabitants. To extend the metaphor, we could think of school as a reproductive act. The adult culture defines itself in curricular terms that it seeks to instill into the next generation, gathered into classroom groups. Let's explore classroom management in this context through two intriguing contradictory perspectives, each with considerable support in our society.

The Classroom as a Womb

The school year in the United States is about 9 months long, which is about the gestation period of a human fetus. A womb is a warm, supportive, nutritionally controlled environment. The embryo/fetus doesn't make any of the conscious decisions during the pregnancy, although in time the mother can sense its responses to what's occurring and possibly adjust things. It's in the mother's best interests to be responsible in decisions that affect her pregnancy. To injure her developing fetus through the use of nonmedicinal drugs, for example, results in a harsh biological judgment and punishment—she must rear the child she injured.

Many people think of a classroom as something like a nurturing womb, a controlled environment in which an immature social organism (the class) gradually develops toward the more independent level of birth (the class graduates). An instructional umbilical cord that connects society to the classroom supplies the needed curricular *nutrients* during development.

This perspective suggests that students are by definition immature in important knowledge and skills, and so it is in society's and the students' best interests for the teacher to carefully control the classroom environment, to shield students from the harsh education they would get if they had to get it all on their own within the community. For example, classroom walls keep immature students from wandering cluelessly in the traffic. This perspective sees formal education as an expensive and significant element of enculturation and argues that our society can't afford to make errors in its operation by encouraging or allowing immature students to control things. Even Dewey (1938), the founder of Progressive Education, argued that it was foolish to assign mature adults to work in classrooms with immature students and then not to use their maturity to enhance the students' experience.

In such an adult-controlled nurturing setting, the class (as a dependent social organism) can develop positively in its knowledge and skills over the 9-month school year and emerge from its classroom womb on a spring day into the birth of a joyful independent summer vacation. Three months later, groups of students will crawl back into another classroom womb, repeat the process, and mature a little more. They will eventually graduate and become autonomous productive adults.

The Class as an Independent Social Organism

Not so, argue the critics of the classroom-as-a-womb perspective. These critics don't consider a class to be a dependent entity but rather a living, functioning social organism, and they believe that the classroom setting should encourage the free exploration of much of what life is about. Such a class was conceived as a social organism in the principal's office in late summer from the school's genetic pool (the student files) and was born the day after *Labor* Day (in many communities) to live a rich 9-month life. The class will inevitably die as a social organism on the final day of school, with practically no chance of coming together again intact in subsequent school years. A class has a 9-month life and a charge to make the most of it.

Developing social and democratic skills is a principal task of the school, and so this perspective argues that the school should encourage a class to collaboratively chart its own social and problem-solving development as much as possible. It should discover how to make the best use of each student, just as our bodybrain must get all its organs and systems to function collaboratively.

We could thus think of the school year as a lifetime that includes an early autumn childhood in which the class begins to feel its own way with a lot of encouragement and support from the teacher (just as parents play a similarly important role in a child's early maturation). We could think of the extended middle months as analogous to a productive adult life in which the group assumes much more control over its affairs. We could think of the spring months as analogous to the senior, more reflective years of life. It's an opportunity to look back to see how far we've come and what we've accomplished. In a classroom group, this period can become an important time for individual students to solidify relationships and to set their agenda for subsequent years. Who was I? Who am I? Who will I become?

This collaborative classroom management perspective argues that the only way for students to master social and problem-solving skills is to explore and practice them with as much independence as possible. To have the teacher and curriculum teach these skills via lesson format isn't as powerful as having students discover and experience them, and as long as the teacher monitors such issues as safety and legality, the classroom orientation should be to collaboratively foster social and problem-solving independence. The teacher must obviously play the same protective role that a parent plays during infancy, to help get the group started. But once the school year is under way, the teacher should take every possible opportunity to let the class group determine its own way, to identify and solve its own social problems. This perspective strongly believes in the ancient adage that the teacher *must* decrease in importance over time so that the students *may* increase.

So which perspective is correct? When we look to biology for guidance, we can see support for a nurturing dependency—the coverings around nuts, bird nests to shelter eggs covered by eggshells, the chrysalis covering of the insect pupal stage, the mammalian womb. We can also see support for early exploratory independence; most animals are on their own shortly after birth, innately tuned to survival in the environment in which they'll live.

A womb-like classroom's strengths are in helping students to discover in successive settings what others think of them, how the environment shapes them, and how to function appropriately within a group. Its goal is to get the class through the year's curricular expectations.

A collaborative classroom's strengths are in helping students to discover what they and others think, how they can best shape their own classroom environment, and how they can best evolve as a functioning group. Its goal is to get the class simply to collaboratively experience the year for what it is.

The goals seem contradictory, but many teachers try to combine them. For example, they take a nurturing *womb* approach during skill development activities (such as in reading and in math computation) and a *collaborative* approach during such activities as the arts and humanities and planning classroom events.

Problems emerge. What happens if students go through a year in which their teacher encourages them to work together on many things, and they develop the skills of independent social action—and the following year most are assigned to a teacher who tightly controls classroom life? What happens when a new student joins a class that has spent months developing a productive collaborative group identity, and the new student has difficulty in participating in such activities? What happens in a school in which the staff prefers the collaborative perspective, but students come and go so much that the spring student body is considerably different from the previous fall? Furthermore, students in a departmentalized school may experience a range of management perspectives during the course of a single day because the staff differs significantly in their beliefs about classroom management (something easily discovered when a staff discusses these two perspectives and then votes their personal orientation).

Although this book is obviously biased toward a collaborative classroom management model, it's important to realize that one can make a very good case for either perspective, and both perspectives have considerable support within our profession and among our patrons.

It's also important to realize that citizens in a democracy continually shift in their level of autonomy across the day. They perhaps determine morning prework activities autonomously, work for an autocratic boss, collaboratively decide where to eat lunch with associates, assign their children afterschool household chores, and participate in a collaborative civic task force in the evening. So don't let it bother you too much if part of a student's school experience is collaborative and part is authoritarian. So goes life.

Use the above metaphor for personal contemplation and also in staff discussions about whether the teacher or students should make the principal energy expenditure in determining classroom management decisions (initially and across the school year). For example, how important is consistency throughout the day in a classroom or within an entire school? Unfortunately, metaphors are much better at defining problems than at providing easy solutions, but they do enhance the discussions that lead to solutions, and I certainly wish you well in that important initial exercise. Think bottom-up. Begin with something that makes sense to you and your class and go on from there.

FROM POTENTIAL TO KINETIC ENERGY

The issue of who should expend the energy to determine and execute classroom management policies and procedures might depend, at least to some extent, on the nature and wishes of individual students and the nature of the class group. One could argue that students who are quite immature would need more professional direction than more mature students. Conversely, an elementary class with 1,000 hours over 9 months at its disposal has more time to gradually develop and determine its social organization than a secondary school departmentalized class that meets only 45 minutes a day for 12 weeks (about 45 hours). One can also argue (as this book does) that since we're born into a democratic society, the process of collaborative management should be introduced as early as possible, to the extent that it's possible.

The collaborative issue occurs at all school levels. As both student and teacher, I can recall marvelous graduate seminars in which the students organized and ran the course, and I can recall being a student in marvelous courses in which I didn't want to spend class time on such management issues but rather preferred to assimilate as much as possible of the professor's superior knowledge of a subject that I wanted to master. I also know that not all students in a given graduate seminar want to run things, and not all students in a lecture course want to be lectured at, even by a superstar in the field.

So it might come down to the simple question of what part of the school experience emotionally arouses (or challenges) a student. Emotion and attention are our activation systems, and Chapter 3 suggested that arousal is mediated by the effects of long-term temperament, short-term mood, and immediate emotional needs—a rich stew pot indeed.

As indicated earlier, we are a social species, continually cooperating and competing with each other. We are stimulated by activities that involve both—for example, in business by debate and negotiation, in play by games such as basketball and bridge. What determines when we prefer to use our energy to compete or to collaborate? The answer emerges partly out of our human ability to assess others and ourselves in social situations and so determine the personal payoff for competition or collaboration. Recent evolutionary psychology research on aggressive behavior and the related concepts of self-concept (how I define myself) and self-esteem (how I value that definition) provide an intriguing biological perspective of the possible source of a student's desire to positively participate in or to negatively oppose the collaborative management of a class.

So in the discussion that follows, think of self-concept/self-esteem as a basic energizing force that helps to drive emotion (which drives attention, problem solving, and behavior). It's therefore something that we need to understand as we wrestle with the issue of who should manage the classroom—and how to initiate and execute a collaborative model.

SELF-ESTEEM, IMPULSIVITY, AND AGGRESSION

Impulsive behavior can lead to reckless behavior, which can lead to violently aggressive behavior. Thus many personal and social problems begin with an impulsive act that is triggered (at least in part) by the aggressor's level of self-esteem.

Our extended maturation and relatively long life span turned us into an interdependent social species. We are thus rightly concerned that efforts and resources are equitably distributed within our formal and informal groups and that hostility among members is minimized. We compete for individual success with the available resources, but our individual success often depends on our ability to function collaboratively within the social hierarchy of the group.

Two intriguing questions focus on how our cognitive systems developed to solve such social management problems: (1) How did our brain develop its ability to function effectively and contentedly within a hierarchical social setting, and (2) which brain systems regulate and trigger our variable social responses, from altruism to aggression?

These are important societal and classroom management questions because if genetics and biochemical systems combine to trigger aggression, for example, one could argue that chronically aggressive people have a reduced capacity for free will and thus should not be held as responsible for their acts as others are. Furthermore, if courts mandate (and/or schools encourage) medical treatments for people who behave inappropriately, the policy could be viewed as governmental *mind control,* racism, or elitism. The social implications of this research and the policies that will emerge out of it are profound and wide ranging. For example, when determining legal or classroom responsibility for an aggressive act, should we simply consider the behavior to be wrong, or should we factor in negative effects of the aggressor's life experiences and environment and the specific event(s) that triggered the aggression?

Brain Systems

Our modular brain's complex collections of neural networks process our cognitive activity. Individual networks that process specific functions combine to process more complex functions. Several dozen neurotransmitter and hormonal systems provide the key chemical substrate of this marvelous information-processing system. Neurotransmitter molecules produced within one neuron are released from its axon (output) terminal into the synaptic gap, where they cross over and attach to (input) receptors on the dendrites or cellular surface of the next neuron in the information sequence. Each neuron produces one or two types of neurotransmitter.

Recent studies with human and nonhuman primates suggest that fluctuations in the availability of the neurotransmitter serotonin play an especially important role in regulating our level of self-esteem and our place within the social hierarchy. Researchers associate high serotonin levels with high self-esteem and social status and low serotonin levels with low self-esteem and status. Behaviorally, high serotonin levels are associated with the calm assurance that leads to smoothly controlled movements, and low serotonin levels are associated with the irritability that leads to impulsive, uncontrolled, reckless, aggressive, violent, suicidal behaviors that are often directed to inappropriate targets. Serotonin levels also seem to affect attention deficit (ADD, ADHD) and other movement-related school behavioral disorders.

It's adaptive for a social species to develop a system that arranges groups into reasonably compatible hierarchical arrangements to better perform various group tasks (and especially those over evolutionary time that enhanced skilled movements). The entire group benefits if survival-related tasks are assigned to those who are generally recognized to be the most capable. As indicated above, self-concept thus emerged to provide us with a sense of how we define ourselves relative to others, and self-esteem emerged to determine how we value that definition. These judgments help us to determine our strengths and weaknesses and encourage us to strive within the group. Consider the personal and skill factors involved in the choice sequence when children choose up sides for teams. They quickly learn the social importance of movement skills.

R. Wright (1995) suggested that the social feedback we get from our actions creates fluctuations from our basal serotonin levels, and this helps us to determine our current level of self-esteem. Thus serotonin fluctuations are adaptive in that they help primates to negotiate social hierarchies, move up as far as circumstances permit, and be reasonably content at each stage. Social success elevates our self-esteem (and serotonin levels), and each such success further raises our social expectations, perhaps to try for a promotion or leadership role we hadn't considered when we were lower on the hierarchy.

A biological system of variability in self-esteem prepares and encourages us to reach and maintain a realistic level of social status, given our abilities and the group's composition. A high or low level of self-esteem (and serotonin) isn't innate and permanent. Very successful people may tumble precipitously in social status, self-esteem, and serotonin levels when they retire or are discharged, thereby experiencing a rapid reduction in positive social feedback.

This doesn't mean that the serotonin system developed to help low-status people endure their fate for the common good. Evolutionary psychology argues that natural selection rarely designs things for the good of the group. The serotonin system rather provides us with a way to cope psychologically in a bad social situation—to be content to play a group role that is consistent with one's current limitations.

The *Peter Principle* wryly argues that bureaucracies generally suffer from a high level of incompetence since employees tend to be promoted one level beyond their level of competence. At that point, promotions cease because of negative performance feedback, and the tenured employee settles into a career of barely getting by until retirement.

Males (normatively) seem to value competition and the development and maintenance of social hierarchies more than females. Although it's currently an ill-understood issue, evolutionary psychologists suggest that this tendency may have emerged out of gender differences in reproductive needs and strategies and possibly out of the role differentiation of hunting parties, but gender group differences don't predict the behavior of individual males and females. The human serotonin system seems to function similarly in males and females in the important roles it plays in regulating self-esteem and aggression control.

The Roots of Violence and Aggression

Violent and aggressive acts are very distressing to the victims and are prominently featured in the news and mass media, but they aren't the norm in social interactions. Furthermore, young males commit most such acts, and 7% of the population commits 80% of the acts. Thus violence and aggression are a limited social pathology, one that evolutionary psychologists seek to explain. Consider the following scenario: a young man goes out for football in his freshman high school year. He's thrilled just to make the team, even though he knows he's low in the hierarchy and won't get to play much in games. He's content for now because he also knows that the coaches and his teammates will note every successful act he makes in scrimmage, and so his playing time will come.

Evolutionary psychology argues that each success enhances his serotonin level and so also his motor coordination and self-esteem. He moves up the team hierarchy, substituting for a few minutes in games. His competition for most of his journey isn't the *alpha males* at the top of the hierarchy but rather those who are competing with him for the next slot in the team hierarchy. Over several years, his talent and that of his teammates will determine the level he achieves. He may thus settle for 4 years of comradeship, scrimmage, and limited game time because he realizes that's where he properly fits into the team hierarchy, or he may eventually bask in the celebrity afforded to him as one of the team stars. If the latter, he may begin the sequence anew in a college team and then perhaps again in a professional team. If the former, his memories and friendships will have to suffice, and he will seek success in other social areas.

But what if he believes that he's better than others who get to play more, but the coaches don't agree and won't give him a proper chance to play? Perhaps it's because of something he can't control (such as his height), or else he believes that his main competitor for his position gets to play more because he's the son of the coach's best friend. Imagine his frustration and rage. His opportunities don't match his sense of self. Consider also how people feel when such artificial factors as gender, race, ethnicity, and age (rather than ability) are used to limit their competitive potential in a wide range of social and vocational settings.

Evolutionary psychologists suggest that this cognitive drive to move into our expected slot in the hierarchy is so strong that many will do whatever it takes to achieve success. If the frustration becomes too intense, a person may act impulsively, recklessly, or stupidly for any possible chance of success, and such reflexive risk taking may on occasion escalate into aggressive and violent acts. A world-class figure skater even attempted to ensure her status by conspiring to injure the knees of a rival highly ranked Olympic Games competitor.

When young people find themselves in a situation in which they see no hope to rise within mainstream society, they may create their own hierarchical gang cultures (and classroom cliques) that provide them with opportunities to succeed within their counterculture's mores. Those among the mainstream successful who decry gang symbols and exclusionary turf areas should look to the high-status symbols they use to flaunt their success, as well as to their exclusionary golf courses and walled communities. Are our society's mainstream culture and counterculture that different biologically in terms of a need for a positive self-concept and self-esteem—for recognition that they are *players* in important areas of their life?

In primate groups with a developed stable hierarchy, those at the bottom (who had little control over events) experienced far more stress and stress-related illness than those at the top. Conversely, during periods in which the hierarchical structure was unstable and shifting, those currently at the top (whose power was threatened) experienced the most stress and stress-related illness (Sapolsky, 1999). Thus it's in the interest of the power elite (in community and classroom) to maintain social stability, and it's in the interest of the currently disenfranchised to create as much social instability (and classroom disruption) as possible in a desperate search for respect and success. Does this assessment match the group of students in your class who have been the principal behavior problems?

The fewer opportunities young people have to succeed in mainstream society and the classroom, the more social instability we can expect. It's not in our nation's interest to support exclusionary policies that limit social goals and to reduce the powerful role that schools play in helping students to seek their dreams. A collaborative classroom can be an important laboratory for enhancing students' beliefs that they are mastering the social skills they'll need to succeed in a complex society. A collaborative management model may thus be of greatest importance for those who feel the most rejected.

I listened to talk radio stations during a 2-hour drive the other day. I couldn't help but notice how many tightly constricted voices came on to express their outrage over something or other. They obviously felt disenfranchised in a society that ignores their concerns. They call in to talk radio shows because they get a few minutes to tell perhaps the entire country how distressed they are about whatever distresses them (generally, the government). How sad that their school experiences didn't provide them with useful civic participation skills. They've become anonymous voices on talk radio rather than effective participants on civic committees focused on their concerns. Imagine what 12 years of collaborative classroom management could have done for such folks. They might still be outraged, but at least they would have learned how to effectively express themselves and how to directly participate in civic governance.

The Role of Drugs and Nutrition

Is it possible to chemically jump-start the serotonin system when conditions have become so averse in a person's life that self-esteem and serotonin levels have plummeted into the depths of depression? Fluoxetine antidepressant drugs such as Prozac, Zoloft, and Paxil can do this. When neurotransmitters leave an axon terminal, they attach to a receptor on the receiving neuron and pass on the sending neuron's chemical message. Most are then reabsorbed into the axon terminal and used again. Drugs such as Prozac block the *reuptake channels* on the terminal and so slow the reabsorption process. This means that the serotonin neurotransmitters in the synapse may activate several times before being reabsorbed, and so fluoxetine drugs increase the effectiveness of a limited discharge of serotonin without actually increasing the amount in our brain.

This somewhat artificial chemical elevation often enhances a person's motor competence and self-esteem, and this increased optimism and happier mood lead to the positive social feedback that allows the natural system to take over again in time and to function more effectively. Think of jump-starting a dead car battery—a few miles of driving will reenergize the battery, and it can then function on its own.

When researchers physically removed the dominant male from a troop of vervet monkeys and gave fluoxetine antidepressant drugs to a randomly selected lower ranking male, that male assumed a dominant role (Nesse & Williams, 1994).

Such herbal remedies as St. John's wort may successfully elevate serotonin levels in people whose levels are moderately low.

People often use alcohol when they feel low, and alcohol does release more serotonin into the synapses. It can thus temporally help to raise one's mood and self-esteem, but chronic alcohol use depletes a brain's store of serotonin, and so it makes matters even worse by further impairing the impulse control system.

Nutrition may provide another avenue to serotonin elevation. Serotonin is derived from the amino acid *tryptophan*. Carbohydrates enhance the entry of tryptophan into our brain. Prolonged periods of stress increase our brain's need for serotonin. Nutrition researchers have discovered a connection between serotonin/carbohydrate levels and emotionally driven eating disorders that emerge out of family stress, premenstrual syndrome, shift work, seasonal mood changes, and the decision to stop smoking. Wurtman and Suffes (1996) proposed nondrug diet adaptations that could solve some of these problems.

It's interesting that we humans have long self-medicated ourselves with alcohol and carbohydrates (sweets and starches) to temporarily and artificially boost our self-esteem—and Friday afternoon margaritas and chips after a difficult, depressing week seemingly provide a double boost.

From Positive Social Feedback to Classroom Management

Prescription and other drugs can provide only a temporary chemical boost in the energy of self-esteem, and diets require a certain level of self-control. The best support for a serotonin deficiency is probably the natural system of activity and positive social feedback that we have evolved over millennia. Werner and Smith (1992) have conducted a four-decade longitudinal study of seriously at-risk children who matured into resilient successful adults. The authors found that they received unconditional love from family and/or non-family mentors, who encouraged their curiosity, interests, and dreams and who assigned them responsibilities that helped them to discover their strengths and weaknesses.

Kays (1990) discovered that an important factor in the alienation from school that many at-risk students in Grades 4 and 5 were beginning to feel occurred because their teachers didn't involve them in many routine classroom tasks. Other students were asked to water the plants and get things from the office—but not the at-risk students. How can students learn responsibility if they're not asked to be responsible in simple chores related to classroom management?

If both an inexperienced substitute football player and the team's star can work together comfortably and effectively, a collaborative classroom spirit can similarly become a powerful energizing tool for helping a class to enhance their collective self-concept/self-esteem. Leadership roles constantly shift as students with special skills assume important roles when their skills are needed. In the football metaphor above, place kickers spend most of the game on the sidelines. It doesn't bother them because they know that they will become central to the team when their skills are needed. But they also know they can't succeed unless the other 10 players carry out their responsibilities. That's the essence of collaborative energy—one for all and all for one.

Serotonin research thus adds biological support to educational practices that help develop the skills a class needs to participate responsibly and effectively in the collaborative management of its classroom. The suggestions that follow should encourage staff and students to begin the self-examination and exploration that is needed to determine who should do what.

SUGGESTED ACTIVITIES

Data Gathering

You and your class can gather useful information for class discussions about a variety of collaborative management issues through simple data-gathering activities about such things as how the class feels about something or how much energy an activity took.

Consistently use a simple 5- or 10-point high-low scale to informally gather data (10 or 5 is high, 1 is low, and the other numbers represent intermediate values). Such a scale provides a rapid, honest, and easily computed response range from the entire group, and this provides substance to any discussion about what's occurring or what should occur. If secrecy is important, ask students to write the number that represents their opinion on a small slip of paper, gather the slips, quickly tabulate them on the chalkboard, and collectively analyze the group's response. If secrecy isn't important, ask students to write down the number on any sheet of paper on their desk, and then ask students to hold up their sheet when the tabulator calls out the individual numbers on the scale. (Writing down the number encourages students to stay with their original choice when the scale numbers are called out and not to change an opinion to match a friend's.) Consider the following data-gathering suggestions that move from immediate to extended data gathering, and then work with your class to develop other activities that fit your situation.

• Begin the day or an activity by asking students to indicate how they currently feel (on a good-bad scale) or their energy or interest level (on a high-low scale).

• At the end of an activity or end of the day, ask students to use the scale to indicate how they felt the activity or day went.

• After a written activity, ask students to place a number on the top of the page to indicate how much energy they expended to complete the assignment or how confident they are of their success in completing it, their level of interest in the activity, and so forth. Tabulate the numbers, and begin the next day's discussion of the assignment with a discussion of the results.

• Record student stress levels daily for at least 2 weeks. When students first enter the classroom each day, ask each student to write a number that represents his or her perceived stress level on a piece of paper and then to drop the slip in a box. Place each day's slips in a sealed envelope, labeled with the day. Also keep a daily record of notable events such as weather changes, arguments, and management problems that occurred. After 2 or more weeks, work as a class to tabulate, compute, and graph the daily average results for the entire period. Note and discuss patterns and fluctuations over the period, and use the record of daily events to explain high and low days, variations over a week, and so on. What effect does the morning assessment have on what happens over the course of the day? What might the group do to reduce negative effects? It's important to gather all the data before analyzing any of it so that each day's assessment doesn't affect the next day's assessment during the study period.

In an extended informal middle school study of daily stress levels (that used a 10-point scale), one of my graduate students discovered that the data predicted weather changes (with a large fluctuation in perceived stress levels occurring a day or so before the weather changed). He also found that the scores on a given day tended to converge around the teacher's personal score of the previous day (not surprising, since if a teacher feels stressed on Tuesday, the students won't come to school on Wednesday with a whole lot of optimism).

- Ask three students to sit apart at locations where they can easily observe what's going on. At the conclusion of every minute for an hour, each one should write down a subjective assessment of how much positive energy was collectively being expended in the classroom (10 = *very much,* 1 = *very little*). At the end of the hour, ask them to graph their 60 observations on a graph or graphs that allow for easy comparison. Collectively compare and discuss the three assessments of the same hour.

Using Common Activities to Explore and Enhance Classroom Energy

- When students have many opportunities to work together in groups, they may experience success in both leading and supporting roles, an important developmental consideration for bold/uninhibited and anxious/inhibited temperaments. Positive self-esteem can develop at any level in a work group if the problem is challenging and the group values the contributions of all. The emergence of Cooperative Learning strategies in recent years has provided educators a useful vehicle for helping students to explore and expand themselves.

- Portfolio assessments are another excellent vehicle for encouraging the self-examination in students that enhances their self-concept/self-esteem. Journals, creative artwork, and other forms of reflective thought can produce similar results.

- Many classroom conflicts arise because an impulsive act escalates into aggression. We have tended to view these events only in negative terms—as misbehavior, as something to be squashed. Rather, use positive group strategies to help students study such behavior and discover how to reduce it. Students can then use their own behavior in a classroom laboratory self-study of social behavior.

- Many teachers begin the school year with a somewhat arbitrary posting-of-the-rules that will govern classroom behavior. Another more collaborative approach would be to take the time to list and discuss the wide variety of people who expend energy to determine events and behavior in a complex institution such as a school and then collaboratively seek to determine who should decide what and why.

Title the activity across the top of the chalkboard "Who Decides What and Why?" Under this, horizontally write the following decision-making category levels so that students can suggest and write specific activities under each category (and you can then add things that they don't know or can't think of):

Beyond the Building Level

At the Building Level by Others

At the Classroom Level by the Teacher

At the Classroom Level by Teacher and Students

At the Classroom Level by Individual Students

• Decisions beyond the building level involve such things as laws, personnel decisions, funding, busing, and snow days. General building-level decisions involve such things as lunch, library, and gym schedules; classroom assignments; and aide assignments. Teacher decisions might involve such things as the day's schedule, curricular assignments, desk arrangements, and the condition of the room at the end of the day. Teacher/student decisions might involve such things as class projects and parties. Individual student decisions involve such things as what to read during a free reading period, personal thoughts, and friendships. It's always interesting to discover what a class group will identify.

When the listing is complete, work as a group to identify (with an X) those items that the class feels should be negotiable— things that others typically decide but that they believe should be decided with student input. Then circle those items that the class actually wants to expend the energy to negotiate and/or to control decisions.

It will be an interesting discussion. Your class will discover as they work through the activity that no one person controls all decision making in a school; legal/safety issues, perceived community consensus, available funding, and a variety of other factors also must be considered when making almost all decisions. Even if a teacher insists that a student should do something, *misbehavior* is a term that suggests limitations in teacher authority. It takes a lot of collaborative energy to run a classroom and school, and that's an important lesson to teach and learn at the beginning of the year.

- Videotape technology has developed to the point that it's now relatively easy to videotape class discussions related to conflict resolution. Videotape such discussions several times during the school year. Toward the end of the year, replay selected tapes that demonstrate how the class improved in its ability to conduct such discussions and resolve its differences.

Creating a Collaborative Classroom

Most teachers who have described how they moved toward collaborative classroom management told me that they did it bit by bit (from simple, noncontroversial issues to the more complicated). Many eventually moved toward a classroom governmental organization of sorts that formalized the collaborative model. They used this to resolve issues that are better resolved through a small group rather than via discussion and action by the entire class group.

The typical plan paralleled the local city government with positions (mayor, council, etc.) that parallel classroom functions. Rather than elect officers, teachers typically divided up the year so that all students had an opportunity to hold a position sometime during the year (and students drew slips of paper to discover the position they would hold during their term, a technique that kept the process from becoming a popularity contest).

The class first had to study its city's government to discover what energy, space, time, movement, and range issues the city government resolved. Students then identified analogous classroom issues, and these became the issues the council discussed and resolved while the rest of the class observed the meetings.

The point I want to make is that there's no one way to process the management issues in a collaborative model. The city council approach described above probably wouldn't work in a first grade or in a high school class that only meets for 45 minutes, but it would work well in a self-contained intermediate grade or in a middle school home room. Each teacher and class will have to develop a model that works best for their particular circumstances. I've been impressed by the variety of plans that teachers have described to me. It reinforces my belief that bottom-up innovations work.

CHAPTER FIVE

Collaboratively Managing Biological and Cultural Space

Space is an important cognitive concept—here and there, in and out, up and down, big and little, fat and thin, flat and hilly. We're born capable of learning how to successfully solve basic spatial problems in our immediate environment—how to move toward opportunities and away from dangers—and we spend much of our lives physically and mentally exploring our planet.

Three of Gardner's (1983, 1998) nine forms of intelligence focus on space: *spatial* (visual perception and re-creation abilities), *bodily-kinesthetic* (body motion and navigation abilities), and *naturalist* (object classification abilities). Knowing how to manage space is thus a very important issue for one brain and also for a classroom of bodybrains. For somewhat simple starters, how does a modular brain arrange its various interactive neural networks within its skull, and how does a class arrange its interactive set of living and nonliving things within its classroom?

The more difficult problems are to discover why some brain and classroom spatial elements are curiously arranged and how spatial organization affects behavior. In our brain, for example, conscious body movements are principally initiated by a narrow band of cortex that stretches over our brain from ear to ear. Curiously, the motor cortex section in each hemisphere controls movements on the opposite side of our body, and our body areas are arrayed upside down along the motor cortex (the motor areas at the top of our brain control our feet, and the areas near our ears control facial movement). Strange brain geography!

Classroom geography can also sometimes be strange. An elementary teacher told me that she always gathers her class into a circle at the end of the last school day of the month to discuss how the month had gone and what they might do during the next month. She calls one segment of this session *curiosities,* during which she asks students to identify things that seemed odd, not quite right. She's discovered that periodically someone will identify something reasonably important that she or others hadn't noticed.

One year at the end of October, a student remarked that the teacher had the biggest desk in the room and that it was arranged so that her total area took up a lot of classroom space (as much as several student desks). Furthermore, her desk was located in the best spot in the room (with a great view of the mountains), and yet she rarely used it during the day. So the issue was, in effect, why did she get the most and best real estate in the room and didn't even use it? The teacher had been teaching for years and had never realized what her student had observed. The result was that she immediately asked her class to help her move her desk into the corner with the lowest real estate values, thus freeing up a lot of classroom space. They then worked out a revolving schedule that allowed three students each month to temporarily move into the prime real estate area with the great view.

So brains and classrooms contain spatial curiosities that often pass us by unless we tune in to their possibilities. This chapter will thus suggest ideas, examples, and metaphors related to four spatial aspects of classroom life and management, with the hope that they will spark the kind of data-gathering, discussion, and design activities that will enhance the understanding and collaborative management of classroom space.

1. *Located Space.* Objects occupy space, whether they're neurons in a brain or desks in a classroom. Sometimes location isn't important (such as the location of a single rock in a rocky area), but location is often quite important to the success of living things in highly competitive settings (such as the location of a tree in a forest

or of a café in a business district). The location of a table or a student in a classroom may or may not be important. The general issue of location brings to mind the two classic approaches to housekeeping. The one approach is that there's a logical place for everything, and everything should be in its place; the other is that wherever a thing is, that's where it was destined to be.

2. *Covered Space.* A leaky wall (a semipermeable membrane) generally surrounds a class group. Membranes and their channels (such as classroom walls and doors) participate in the creation of vibrant internal life forces and then disperse the resulting products and behaviors. To *create* something very vibrant within a classroom is different from merely *constructing* it. Constructed things follow an established set of directions, so we can only appreciate them when they're complete, but we can imagine and appreciate created things (such as a class, classroom, curriculum, or school year) before, during, and after their creation. The challenge is to create a stimulating classroom environment within the spatial limitations of an already existing school and its policies.

3. *Organized Space.* Considerable evidence suggests that a stimulating complex social environment enhances the physical development of the cortex, the part of our brain that processes much of the curriculum (Diamond & Hopson, 1998). The nonliving spatial elements of the classroom (such as its walls, furniture, and materials) can also materially enhance the creation of a stimulating environment if the inhabitants imaginatively arrange it.

4. *Shared Space.* Two dozen or so people share a limited class-room space, so classroom management policies and practices should respect everyone's fundamental constitutional right to privacy and due process, as well as our human right to a safe teaching and learning environment.

Teachers who have told me (via course papers and e-mail) about their initial explorations in collaborative classroom management have typically reported that they began with spatial explorations. It makes sense since classroom space is in a constant state of flux. Organizing the space is a pleasant and generally noncontroversial enterprise that engages everyone. If one arrangement doesn't work, it's relatively easy to try something else.

Use the following map activity to help your students visualize the concept of space since maps (and architectural plans, musical scores, equations, etc.) allow us to mentally imagine things that are physically quite complicated. Use available brain scan photographs and aerial photographs of your community (and/or others) to enhance understanding.

MAPPING COGNITIVE, CITY, AND CLASSROOM SPACE

A brain imaging machine looks down on the deeply folded, approximately 3–square foot cortex of our modular brain. It images (identifies) individual brain areas that briefly activate as they participate in processing the cognitive tasks that currently engage the person being imaged (typically using the sequence of colors in the spectrum to register variations in activity in various imaged areas: red = high activity to purple = low activity). Each brain area specializes in a specific aspect of the myriad actions that a brain can carry out, and each area connects to and influences the actions of many other areas, with the aggregate of all the small-to-large activated areas collaborating to process the task at hand. Scientists who study brain scans are learning much about the spatial organization of our modular brain, but the underlying biological logic and management of the system remain elusive (the motor cortex discussed above being an intriguing example).

Now let's think of spending a day hovering over a midsize city in a helicopter. We would note similarities in observing the behavior of 100 billion neurons and 100,000 citizens. From the helicopter, we might first note the smaller lifeless geometric shapes that constitute homes and buildings. But we would also recognize larger, less clearly defined spatial configurations that constitute such things as industrial, business, and governmental areas; shopping malls; and the neighborhoods with their collections of schools, churches, parks, and business/professional areas. We might also be able to determine that some city areas are composed mostly of old buildings and others of new buildings.

Connecting all these smaller and larger spatial entities are the city's inner complex of streets, roads, freeways, and bridges, as well as the rivers, airport, and highways systems that allow things to move in and out of the city. Not visible but important are the underground wires and pipes.

We would note that some intersecting streets don't connect easily and some areas and structures seem curiously misplaced (such as a beautiful, large old church in a now shabby, partially industrial neighborhood). A city's landscape constantly shifts, and since it's difficult to move or redesign some large buildings, it's sometimes best to just adapt things to the current inadequate spatial arrangement—in cities, classrooms, and evolving brains.

During the course of the day, we would note fluctuations in the activity level of various areas and in the arterial ribbons that move people. These might include the morning and afternoon movements between individual homes and the business, industrial, and governmental areas and heightened evening activity in the entertainment and shopping centers. We could assess the amount of activity in a shopping mall, for example, by noting the number of cars parked in its parking lot and the rhythm of a school day by observing such things as the current presence or absence of students in the play areas and the buses out front. The amount of activity an area engenders might be an indication of its importance to the operation of the city.

If we could look closer into all those buildings and track the activity patterns, we would discover that the 100,000 citizens each have an individual permanent home base from which they periodically move to such temporary spaces as school, job, stores, church, and restaurants. So, for example, students with their own room in a shared home spend school days at a private desk in a shared classroom and school, periodically moving to such temporary spaces as a library or cafeteria table. The student's current personal space may also constantly shift, such as during a physical education activity or when moving about the classroom.

Each citizen (or student) is thus an individual space-filling energy module in a city (or classroom) composed of lifeless private and shared space that comes alive when people act and communicate. Folks constantly move here and there to participate in the temporary increase in an area's activity.

City and classroom space utilization thus have intriguing similarities to brain space utilization. Each function in our modular brain occupies its own (localized or distributed) space, but successful brain activity depends on the collaborative and competitive efforts of many brain modules, just as cities and classrooms function best through an appropriate collaborative and competitive mix.

This suggests that a class could profitably imagine the helicopter view of its school and classroom across the school day and study how school space is used to locate and move things. Physical closeness and spatial ownership are two intriguing concepts that will probably emerge during the study, and the suggestions below should assist in the process.

HOW MANY PEOPLE CAN YOU STUFF INTO A CLASSROOM?

Physical Closeness. It's odd, but we'll attend a football game—which is about physical contact—and avoid physical contact with others in attendance, apologizing when accidental contact occurs. We'll crowd into an elevator or bus, but we want different picnic groups to spread out in a park. We'll attend a party in a large house with comfortable conversation-friendly seating areas and all crowd into the kitchen to stand and talk. Men and women happily share the same confined space in a restaurant's eating area but not in its restrooms. People who wouldn't walk around town in a skimpy swimsuit will wear it without embarrassment at a pool. The chances are good that we don't interact much with our neighbors but rather much more with friends who are scattered all over town.

How much space does a class need before friends feel crowded and exhibit the irritation associated with overcrowding? Find out by getting enough moveable partitions to stretch along one classroom wall. Every day move the partitions one foot toward the center of the room (thus reducing the available space in the room). Move desks and other equipment closer together as the room shrinks, and collaborate to gather daily data on how the group is responding (such as recording the number of arguments, daily stress levels, etc.). Discover the point at which the class votes to abandon the project because things have become too crowded. Interestingly, most classes have discovered through the activity that a little crowding isn't necessarily bad if it frees up classroom space that can then be decorated with comfortable furniture, rugs, and plants. Like park space in a city or a living room in a home, it can then be used for activities that are enhanced by the constant availability of the additional space.

Many teachers arrange the classroom furniture to create an open area before the year begins. The difference in doing it this way is that it becomes a *collaborative* exploration. The final arrangement may be similar to what you would have done on your own, but doing it collaboratively is an important step in the development of an orientation toward collaborative classroom management.

Spatial Ownership. We seem to require a sense of defined personal space. Mammals have a powerful tendency to identify, protect, and mark their territory. We observe it when dogs scent trees and shrubs and when homeowners water the hedge on their property line—but perhaps also when the teacher's name is on a classroom door and when folks use knives or aerosol paint cans to tag and claim ownership of someone else's wall. When we wear signed designer clothing, wedding rings, and convention tags, we voluntarily give up a little of our personal spatial identity to someone else.

Elementary students typically have a school space they can call their own—a desk in *their* classroom. Elementary teachers generally involve their students in decorating and caretaker activities that further provide the class with a sense of ownership of personal space. Conversely, secondary school students typically have only temporary desks in a series of teacher-oriented classrooms, and many secondary schools have now even removed the lockers that formerly provided their students with a small personal space in the school.

Personal space is so important to us that many secondary students sit at the same desk every time a class meets and find a place where they can regularly hang out when they're not in class. They may join the school paper staff or some other activity that has a room they can go to, frequent the library (often always sitting at the same table), and/or congregate by their cars in the parking lot or across the street at a convenience store.

The dispossessed in the student body have located no space where they feel a sense of ownership. Is it a surprise that many feel alienated, drop out, and join with their friends to claim ownership of a hang-out space, often in the center of the city (and usually to the intense irritation of nearby businesses)?

We tend not to vandalize our own property, so educators who don't work to create a sense of student spatial identification (or ownership) shouldn't be surprised when students vandalize the school.

Use the scale introduced at the end of Chapter 3 (5 or 10 = *high,* 1 = *low*) to identify the student comfort level with various school areas. Work together to create a form that identifies various school areas (cafeteria, library, office, playground, etc.) and ask students to rate each in terms of how comfortable (safe, happy, etc.) they feel when they are in that area. Tabulate the results and discuss the response patterns, especially those of the areas students rated highest and lowest.

Go beyond the school. Go on a walking field trip into the surrounding neighborhood to discover your students' level of comfort and safety in specific areas and to identify things that enhance and detract from neighborhood safety and attractiveness.

A Classroom Is a Created World Surrounded by a Leaky Wall

Chapter 1 identified the semipermeable membrane as a key biological concept. In the context of this chapter, we can relate that concept not only to our protective skull and our brain's sensory/motor inputs and outputs but also to the classroom's barriers (walls, floor, ceiling) and its openings (door, windows, faucets, heat vents, plug-ins, intercoms, computers, TV set). A classroom's barriers and openings are a rich and delightful exploratory concept for a class intent on understanding and designing its classroom's space.

Barriers. Walls and fences aren't necessarily negative, and neither are the sets of partitions (or barriers) that surround a classroom. They do define the class space and keep out unwanted things. Furthermore, they're fun to contemplate and decorate.

Our clothes and jewelry become decorative extensions of our personalities—communicating facets of ourselves to those who come upon us. Classroom walls and other partitions can similarly become an art gallery of sorts that reflect inwardly upon the inhabitants and helps them to understand who they are and why they are there. Students might appropriately ask the following: Do our classroom walls and partitions exhibit something in progress (creations) or only finished products (constructions)? Do the decorations ask questions or provide answers? Do they stagnate or continually change?

Displays on classroom walls and partitions can become a magic door that opens and psychologically sends students far beyond the classroom (such as pictures of foreign countries), or they can become a barrier door that closes and shuts off questions, choices, and further exploration (such as posted classroom rules). But they can also become a magic mirror that reflects back who the students are and what they might become (such as a display of student poetry).

Chalkboards and projector screens are transitory barriers, windows are transparent barriers, a shelf is a horizontal partition, clothing is a flexible moving partition, a drawer is a hidden barrier, and a ceiling is an interesting barrier to the sky that too few teachers and students explore.

Classroom objects can have multiple uses. For example, we can sit on a table and place something on the seat of a chair. We use a pencil to write on paper, but we can also use it to poke a hole in a sheet of paper or use a sheet of paper to make an origami bird and suspend the bird on a thread from the ceiling.

Openings. Our brain's sensory and motor systems are our brain's in/out channels. What's their classroom equivalent? How do the varieties of things that enter a classroom change before they leave?

We can make classroom objects disappear without using a door or window: put it in a drawer, close the book, roll up the map, turn off the TV, throw it in the wastebasket, close the drapes, erase the chalkboard, drink the water.

A walking field trip around the neighborhood to observe the great variety in buildings, barriers, and openings can lead to interesting and imaginative observations and discussions about the organization and utilization of classroom space. Could a classroom contain the equivalent of a park? Could you increase classroom space through the imaginative use of floor, desktops, shelves, and ceiling (effectively creating a multistory room)? Do rarely used objects need to occupy space that could be used for something frequently used? How many ways can the desks be arranged?

I learned something important about myself and classroom space during my final year as an elementary teacher. I was assigned to be one of the two sixth-grade teachers in a school. During the Labor Day weekend, I followed my custom of elaborately decorating my classroom for the first day of school. For example, I made displays that featured the science and social studies units I planned to teach that year. I developed a bulletin board display of events that occurred during my own sixth-grade year (pictures, magazine covers, etc.). I arranged floral displays. I even stuck golf tees into the ceiling's acoustic tile holes and made an abstract ceiling design out of colored yarn that I looped around the tees. The room was truly impressively inviting.

The other sixth-grade teacher (who had been on the staff the previous year) had to attend a meeting elsewhere that day, and so I looked into his room when I was done and was shocked to see a completely bare room—nothing on the walls or anywhere else. What a cold way to begin the year! I was concerned about our obviously different views of teaching and our potential collegial relationship, having had only a brief perfunctory opportunity to meet him during a formal preschool event.

When school began the next day, I spent the first hour or so describing the coming year through the various displays that I had developed. My students were impressed with what I had done.

By recess I was feeling quite good about myself and grim about my colleague. I walked next door and got the shock of my life. I discovered that when the school day began, my colleague had said in effect that they were all going to be together for a long time and that they would get to know him much sooner than he would get to know each of them (because 25 students observe only one teacher, and one teacher observes all 25 students). So their first assignment was to introduce themselves to him and to their classmates. "Spread yourself along a wall" was the way he put it.

What he had done before they arrived was to attach 30 numbered slips of paper on various room surfaces of different sizes and shapes—surface areas of windows, walls, chalkboards, file cabinets, doors, an area under a table, inside a drawer, and so forth. He asked students to select a numbered area that intrigued them and then sign their ownership of it on a numbered form on his desk.

He then brought out boxes of construction paper, magazines with lots of pictures, wallpaper samples, colored yarn, scissors, marking pens, and masking tape—everything a student might want to develop a display that would be an interesting self-advertisement.

The students obviously loved the assignment, and the room was glorious. The class was indeed spread across most of the room's surfaces. I slunk back into my room in chagrin and confronted myself and my ego trip splattered all over my classroom. My ego was further reduced when my students asked after recess if we could all go next door to "see the really neat things that the other kids did."

I came to peace with myself over time. I came to realize that we were both good teachers who each developed a fine relationship with our students (and with each other). So our different approaches to the first day didn't make or destroy the school year. And I certainly abandoned any sense of sole ownership of our classroom during the rest of the school year as I discovered many ways to do things collaboratively that I had formerly done unilaterally.

So it's OK to create an initial inviting environment that's the equivalent of the coming attraction clips in a film theater. Students do appreciate it when their teacher expends a lot of effort to initially interest them. But it's also important to realize that it's not only the teacher's classroom; rather, it is a room of shared ownership. My decorations were artfully crafted and elegant. The other classroom's decorations were funky, antic, personal, and, alas, also artfully crafted and elegant.

The following year, I went on to complete my graduate program, and so that was my final year as an elementary teacher. I thus didn't have to decide what to do about my classroom at the beginning of the next year (and professors are transients in uniformly dreary university classrooms). Decades later, I believe that a collaborative model is the better alternative but wouldn't criticize a teacher who is currently more comfortable making many unilateral classroom spatial decisions.

A socially stimulating environment will positively affect the physical development of our brain's cortex (Diamond & Hopson, 1998). The challenge is to determine how to create a socially stimulating classroom environment that gets as close as possible to the natural environment to which our brain is innately tuned. Such intriguing questions for a class to explore include the following: At what decorating points does a classroom move from sterile to stimulating to cluttered? Do things that stimulate some students distract others? Which furniture configurations enhance and which detract from social interaction? What is the appropriate relationship between the natural and electronic classroom environment at a time of increased influx of computer technology into the classroom (and into students' lives)? What about those few students who are uncomfortable in a classroom environment that the majority enjoy? This last question especially needs further exploration.

CAULIFLOWER IN THE CLASSROOM

Put a couple dozen people into a room for an extended period, and interpersonal problems related to space utilization will certainly develop. We use terms such as *protected space, territoriality, aggression,* and *predatory behavior* in the larger world, but comfortably shared space is also a genuine classroom management problem. Since it's sometimes easier to understand something by exploring it metaphorically, let's consider student space by imagining the plight of a plant.

Animals beset by predators have appendages that allow them to run, fly, or swim away from danger. Plants have roots that force them to remain where they are and suffer whatever indignities their predators intend—and many students feel similarly rooted to their desks, like plants. So how does a plant protect its personal space?

Over eons, plants have developed several successful defenses against predatory nibbling on their space (such as bark and hard coverings around their fruits). One intriguing plant defense seems to answer the question of why children tend to dislike the vegetables that they often later enjoy as adults, and it also metaphorically suggests a cognitive explanation for some forms of student misbehavior.

Many plants (and especially wild plants) contain toxins, and the toxins differ from plant to plant (Nesse & Williams, 1994). The toxin levels are generally low enough so that they don't kill the animal, but nibbling herbivores will avoid that plant in the future if they find the taste obnoxious and digestion difficult. More commonly, animals diversify their diet to get all the nutrients they need, and so this limits their intake of any one toxin, which, of course, is to the advantage of both plants and animals.

Toxin production uses plant resources that can also be dangerous to the plant, so in general, plant tissues either can have a high level of toxins or grow rapidly, but not both. Rapidly growing and easily replaced plant tissue, such as leaves, would thus have lower toxin levels than the more indispensable plant parts, such as stems and roots. If you have to give up something to herbivores in the ecological battle, give them easily replaced leaves. Although we humans tend to eat a lot of leaves, we also eat the more toxic roots and stems (rather than the leaves) of some vegetables such as carrots, onions, asparagus, broccoli, and cauliflower.

Organisms differ in their susceptibility to toxins. Immature, rapidly growing organisms are generally less able than mature organisms to tolerate toxins. Thus, many children will consider the strong toxin-related odors and flavors of onions, broccoli, and similar vegetables to be obnoxious, while adults consider them spicy and somewhat pleasant.

While children can often successfully (and perhaps honestly) complain to their parents about the bad taste of vegetables, an embryo has a more serious problem. Whatever the mother eats, the embryo eats, and a rapidly growing embryo is especially vulnerable to toxins. The embryonic solution apparently is to send a complaining chemical message to the mother that results in what we commonly call morning sickness. The result is that pregnant women are often nauseated by spicy foods and avoid them, to the benefit of the embryo. Profet (1992) reported that women who don't suffer from pregnancy nausea are more likely to miscarry or bear children with birth defects. (Similarly, pregnant women who use high levels of alcohol or other toxic drugs risk fetal alcohol syndrome and other disorders in their children.)

Even though parents historically didn't actually know that some vegetables have low levels of toxicity that their children can detect, they've intuitively and often successfully used the responsive parental strategy of masking the sharp (toxin) flavors of vegetables to get their children to eat them, such as by placing sugar on carrots and cheese sauce on broccoli and cauliflower.

Whether that's advisable is an interesting issue. Do children who most dislike such vegetables have a lower tolerance for the toxins than children who like vegetables? Can continually forcing children to eat something that nauseates them result in strong negative adult responses, such as the celebrated comment of former President George H. Bush that when he was a child he was forced to eat broccoli and he hated it and that as president of the United States, he reveled in his power to refuse to serve broccoli in the White House? Should children be taught to put up with a little discomfort if the disliked food provides important nutrient values? Is student misbehavior thus a human equivalent to plant toxins?

Our common childhood negative response to vegetables has several interesting classroom parallels in instruction and management. Students similarly respond negatively to difficult-to-process school activities that focus on their bodybrain limitations:

1. *We're born with a brain that's genetically tuned to process such functions as respiration and circulation without any training.* Our

brain is further tuned to the innate recognition of the normal sensory world—infants don't have to learn how to recognize line segments, tones, and smells (although they later have to learn their names). Young children need only limited help to effortlessly master such tasks as the local language and basic arithmetic functions. One reason that the mastery of reading and writing takes years of training and a lot of student effort when oral language was mastered effortlessly is that reading and writing emerged much later than oral language—only several thousand years ago, a relatively short time in terms of our brain's ability to evolve adaptations that combine abstract alphabet lines with speech sounds.

Basic arithmetic processes are similar. Infants can quickly determine such things as the quantity of up to about four items (such as that three items are more than two). Such simple quantity tasks are basic to our survival, so they are built into our cognitive system (Dehaene, 1997). Advanced computational tasks came along later, and so they must be taught and are mastered with difficulty.

The motivation to master these more complex language and mathematical skills comes from the needs of our culture rather than from the natural innate problem-solving needs of a child's brain. We thus shouldn't expect students to be any more pleased by school requirements to master such socially significant skills than they are to eat nutritious foods they don't like but that adults do—because in the adult view, they're good for you.

The classroom itself can be a problem. Children are biologically focused on getting their motor system up to speed. They thus aren't eager to spend 6 hours sitting at a desk in what they consider an uncomfortable environment—exercising only their writing arm. Furthermore, asthmatic children who, for example, are allergic to cats or cigarette smoke are negatively affected by a classroom environment in which nearby students live with cats and smokers and so bring the allergens to school on their clothing.

2. *Our brain is organized so that our strengths often result in weakness in the opposite capability (as in handedness).* For example, our social wary brain has developed excellent conceptualization skills, the ability to rapidly size up and respond to value-laden situations. As indicated in Chapter 3, this survival strength requires a concomitant short attention span and a limited ability to track gradual change and to process details, since giving extended attention to anything would

have made us vulnerable to such dangers as predatory animals creeping up from behind. To put it simply, our brain isn't good at anything that requires solitary sustained attention and precision. Worksheets that require it tend to receive the same grousing that cauliflower and broccoli get at dinner. Our brain has a low tolerance for tasks and settings that natural selection has yet to deem important.

Students tend to respond happily to activities that their brains developed to do well, such as exploring concepts, discovering patterns, estimating and predicting, cooperating on group projects, and discussing moral and ethical issues. Conversely, classroom misbehavior tends to emerge out of factually driven memorizing assignments that require solitary sustained effort and precision.

We tend to sugarcoat such activities, just as we sugar the carrots to make them palatable. We play multiplication tables relay games, run spelling bees, and give prizes for high achievement—all to get students' minds off their cognitive weaknesses, to pretend that such learning doesn't need to come with effort. A concern we'll have to confront is whether making something enjoyable in school is always a good idea. Would we be better off to simply level with students that some culturally important cognitive capabilities require conscious effort and practice to develop?

Conversely, forcing students to spend their days in an uncomfortable classroom environment to master information and skills they don't consider relevant can result in a lifelong aversion to history, math, or whatever. The adult George H. Bush is intelligent enough to realize that broccoli would enhance his diet, but he still dislikes it.

Biologically protective defenses (such as those of cauliflower) suggest that personal territoriality and its protection are important concerns when we attempt to design a single comfortable classroom environment for an entire group that's made up of individuals with separate needs and interests. To develop democratic values in a class means that the minority must accept the will of the majority (which is what legislation and elections are about) but also that the majority must respect the individual rights of the minority (which is what the courts are about). It's often difficult for a class and teacher (with veto power) to democratically resolve classroom spatial issues, just as it's often difficult for governments to develop acceptable regulations about such issues as land use and building exteriors. But such collaborative explorations of how best to arrange and share classroom space during the school years will pay dividends when students mature into citizens who must decide how to arrange and share political space.

It's important to realize that school space issues go well beyond furniture. Schools occasionally get caught up in no-win situations with imaginative students and dress codes (clothing being a spatial phenomenon somewhat akin to building exteriors and signs). Some middle school students wore the T-shirt of a rock band whose name included a word that could be considered obscene. The principal asked the students to turn their shirts inside out and then, to quell such situations in the future, announced on the PA system that students wouldn't be allowed on campus with T-shirts that contained the names of musical groups.

A couple days later, several imaginative students defiantly showed up in T-shirts supporting the local symphony orchestra, fully intent on contacting the local media if they weren't allowed to show their support of a local *musical group*. It was a major embarrassment for the principal.

This is an example of a spatial issue that should have been solved collaboratively. A student/staff discussion about a genuine issue that involved both free speech and public space would at least help students to understand the complexity of spatial issues. It also would have probably resulted in a better resolution than the illogical unilateral decision to equate a specific (possible) obscenity with such a general term as *musical groups*.

Issues such as these remind me of the plight and probable destiny of a dandelion plant in the middle of a bright green lawn. It has a beautiful yellow flower, and the plant itself can be used in salads and to make wine. Children love to blow off and so spread its ball of hundreds of seeds. What more could one want of a simple plant than beauty, food, wine, and entertainment? But we homeowners typically consider it a weed that must be eradicated because we want the lawn to be uniformly green. We tend to believe that colorful flowers (and only hybrids, please) belong in the flowerbed next to the green lawn. It's the botanical equivalent of the racist, sexist, elitist view that "you don't belong here if I didn't select you."

And that's why helping students to discover the shared dynamics of classroom space is an important continuing part of classroom management. The activities suggested throughout this chapter and in the section that follows should initially help students to simply become more aware of space, especially the space the group occupies, and this enhanced awareness should lead to the genuinely shared appropriate and imaginative use of school space.

SUGGESTED ACTIVITIES

A Special Place

Young people today spend a lot of time carefully observing the 1–square-foot, remarkable, brightly colored, rapidly fluctuating electronic world of TV, video games, and computers. Video game success requires an intense functional knowledge of seen and unseen electronic objects that flit about the screen. Surfing the Internet requires the ability to simultaneously manipulate a wide variety of electronic environments, only one of which is immediately visible.

The natural biological world that students also inhabit has its own slower rhythms, and young people should also carefully explore it. The following activity does. Introduce it, and see how far you can take it. Don't worry that not everyone will get into the spirit of the activity and stay with it. Allow it to evolve over time with those who tune into it.

Ask each student to identify an exploratory space in the natural world that's about the size of a TV screen and then to regularly observe it. Possibilities include a marked-off home garden or lawn area, an aquarium, and an ant nest. But it's also OK to go beyond such limitations and observe such things as a family pet or baby sibling, the view out a bedroom window, an outdoor shrub or indoor plant, a seat in a nearby mall, a set of backyard squirrels, or what-ever seems interesting.

Ask students to set up a regular 15-minute period to quietly observe the site and record what occurs. It could be a daily observation or done only several times a week, but it's important to keep a regular schedule that a student can easily remember and maintain.

Ask students to develop a journal to record their observations, a page for each 15-minute period (typing observations into a computer file is OK, but it somehow seems curiously out of the spirit of the activity). The observation episodes tend initially to focus on measurements—how many leaves does the plant have, how many people walked by the mall bench, and how many insects visited the area. Students will create maps that trace the paths of the crawling infant, the family pet, or the aquarium fish and sketch pictures of organisms in the area.

Students will soon move toward more subtle observations, noting changes that occurred between observation episodes, wondering about things that have disappeared, and making predictions of what might occur. Magnifying glasses, tape recorders, and cameras emerge as students dig deeper into and improve their understanding of their small segment of the biological world.

As the project continues, ask students to report on interesting things they've discovered, and encourage the class to seek parallels between (1) their microworlds and the larger world (and especially their classroom) and (2) the electronic world they're also exploring daily.

Preparatory Activities

What follows are some activities that you might use as a lead-up to the "Special Place" project above. Much of the passing scene fortunately bypasses our conscious attention. Imagine the cognitive overload if we were consciously aware of everything in our environment. Still, we often ignore things we should consciously attend to, and so the following activities will lead to interesting discussions about what we tend to notice and don't notice in our environment.

• Ask your students to recall and then sketch what's on a currently nonvisible school wall they see daily (the school entrance, a cafeteria wall, etc.). Then ask them to look only toward the front of the classroom and to sketch what's on the wall behind them. Quietly ask a student to temporarily leave the room, and then ask the class to write descriptions of the student's outer clothing (type of garment, color, etc.). Ask your students to draw two large circles on a sheet of paper and then to sketch in (or use words and arrows to identify and locate) the four different elements on each side of a penny—a coin they handle frequently. Tabulate and discuss the results of such tests. For example, why did some students do better than others, and why did students do better on some tests than on others?

• Speech allows us to create sound representations of visual phenomena—which can be helpful during a telephone conversation— but words often can't easily convey what our visual system sees.

Place a common object such as a pair of scissors, a comb, or a sock in a box so students can't see it. Ask a student to look in the box and to use less than a minute to describe the object, without naming it or indicating its use. Ask the rest to write what they think it is, and discuss the results. What descriptive words or phrases helped the most and the least? Repeat the activity several times with different describers and objects to see if the descriptions and scores improve over time. Use this activity to help prepare your students for the journal they will keep in the "Special Place" project.

• We use all our senses to orient ourselves in space, and so it's interesting to reduce the sensory information and discover if students can still identify something. Tape-record several common school sounds (such as a flushing toilet, the push bar on the front door, a drinking fountain, a playground swing, or the sounds in the office, cafeteria, or gym). Play the tape to discover how many students can identify and/or locate the sound. Do the same thing with smell by placing objects with distinctive odors (such as the school soap, a piece of some of today's lunch, crayons, chalk) in opaque glass containers with holes punched into the lid. Ask students to sniff and identify. Shoot slides of a small segment of a variety of large school areas (such as part of the front door, the classroom ceiling, the cafeteria counter, the side of a school bus). Show the slides and ask students to identify the space. Use these activities to encourage multisensory observations in the "Special Place" project.

• Color plays an important role in our perception of space. If the classroom has a window that the sun shines through, paste various colored cellophane shapes on the window and note the colored patterns that move across the room during the day. Bring some light fixtures to school and place different-colored light bulbs in them. String colored Christmas lights. Place several colored slips of paper in a box, and take one out each Friday before dismissal. Then see how much of that color you and your students can introduce into the room during the next week. Suppose you drew out blue one Friday. Display pictures in which blues dominate. Get some plants with blue flowers. Feature blue in bulletin board displays. Encourage students to wear blue clothing (and line them up from the lightest to darkest blue).

CHAPTER SIX

Collaboratively Managing Biological and Cultural Time

Time is an elusive concept that we tend to view as a cultural commodity. We spend, save, and use time. We consider it precious but often waste it. Children earn free time and are punished with time-out. We're early, late, or about on time. Time flies and drags as it moves us from the past to the present and into the future. We're having the time of our life. Our time is up. In short, time is nature's way of keeping everything from happening all at once.

Our brain oddly has no specific system to recognize and regulate time, even though we function within a large number of important cycles, rhythms, and sequences, such as those that regulate sleeping and waking, feelings of hunger and satiation, and sex hormone distribution. The Premacks (2003) suggested that time is an example of a concept weak in sensory experience that metaphorically borrows meanings from such concepts as space that are rich in sensory experience. For example, we infer time from the distance we traveled or the work we completed. We estimate age by observing someone's body.

We can experience time as being discrete (a series of specific events) or as continuous (a sequence of events that flow together into something we will later recall simply as a *wedding*). Time can exist as an objective chronological sequence of clock ticks and calendar dates, or it can be subjectively flexible (how long it seems to take for a red light to change or a boring activity to end). We tend to automatically wake up at about the same time every morning, and many people awaken briefly from a dream at approximately 3 a.m. School time is about schedules, lesson lengths, grade sequences, due dates, waiting, and much more.

Three of Gardner's (1998) nine forms of intelligence focus on time and sequence: *linguistic, musical,* and *logical-mathematical* intelligences. How are these related to time/sequence? All exploit a marvelous biological principle that allows an organism to use a small number of discrete coding elements to pack an incredible amount of complex information units into a limited biological space. The principal: code the information into the sequence of a relatively small number of separate elements and the length of the coding chain rather than into the elements themselves.

So to revisit and expand the discussion in Chapter 2, we've created an English language of 500,000 words out of 26 letters (or 45 phonemes) by inserting the meaning of a word into its letter sequence and length rather than into the individual letters themselves (such as with *do, dog, god, good,* and *goods*). We can similarly create an infinite number of melodies out of various sequences of the 12 tones in the musical scale and a very complex numerical/mathematical system out of 10 digits (321 not being the same as 123). Imagine the huge amount of brain space we would need to store and process our complex language, music, and mathematical systems without this efficient coding system.

We can further string words into a sentence, sentences into a paragraph, and a sequence of events into a story (and storytelling in its various forms occupies much of our life). Left-hemisphere logical thought processes and established routines tend to focus on what we will do first, second, third, and so forth and why we will follow that particular sequence.

It's intriguing (and somewhat mystical) that the genetic coding system of all organisms also functions similarly, sequentially. The nucleus of every cell in our body contains a yard-long, 50 trillionths of an inch wide, ladder-shaped, deeply folded, identical string of DNA (deoxyribonucleic acid), the *recipe book* for manufacturing cellular materials and regulating cellular processes. Twenty amino acids constitute the ingredients for all plant and animal protein synthesis, and the DNA sequence of a gene (the recipe for constructing a protein) is the sequence of amino acids and the length of the amino acid chain that creates the protein. So we use several sequential *language* coding systems to communicate within one generation and a similarly organized *genetic* coding sequence to create and maintain the children who will become the next generation.

How to appropriately manage the sequence of events that we experience as *time* is thus an important human challenge, so teachers and students should seek to understand and explore time and its various dynamics in both classroom and life management.

This chapter introduces and discusses three human time/ sequence concepts that have rich exploratory possibilities for a creative class interested in the concept of collaborative classroom time management: (1) life span, especially the first two decades of life; (2) time allocations during a school year; and (3) time allocations during an average preadult day.

LIFE SPAN: TWO DEVELOPMENTAL DECADES

A key element of the concept of a life span is that we're a dependent social species, quite helpless at birth, with a brain one-third its adult size. Our approximately 20-year developmental trajectory includes (1) a very dependent childhood decade during which our parents and other adults provide an important protective barrier and needed instruction while our bodybrain systems come on line and (2) a less protected adolescence decade during which the systems mature to the generally effective level of adult life.

Each decade follows a similar general pattern of an initial 4-year period (birth to age 4 and ages 11 to 14) in which the appropriate developmental knowledge and skills typically develop slowly and awkwardly. These initial periods are followed by a 6-year period (ages 5-10 and ages 15-20) characterized typically by a systematic movement toward confident competence in the appropriate knowledge and skills. This 4- to 6-year/4- to 6-year developmental rhythm is incorporated into the typical preschool (4 years), kindergarten through elementary school (6), middle school (4), and high school/college (6) pattern.

Adult life signals a role shift as we become the caretakers of the next generation of dependent children through the direct challenge of parenthood and/or the more indirect challenge of paying taxes and contributing to charities to help support dependent citizens. Finally, adults who live long enough often revert back to a dependent status through family and governmental support systems.

Childhood

During the years from birth to age 10, our developmental focus is on learning how to be a *human being*—learning to move, communicate, and behave appropriately in social settings. These often require the mastery of learned social and cultural conventions, traditions, and rituals and include mastering the movements associated with various games, the differences in various spoken and written languages, and our culture's definition of good manners. Despite what critics say, most children generally function at a reasonably rapid automatic (reflexive) level in childhood motor, language, and social knowledge and skills by age 10. They may not always *do* what they're supposed to do, but they typically know what to do and are capable of doing it.

As indicated above, the initial birth to age 4 development of these abilities is typically slow and awkward, and so it generally occurs at home with a supportive family. Adults generally allow young children to make many mistakes as they stumble to the mastery of basic human skills and knowledge. We smile indulgently and offer support rather than criticism as toddlers trip and 2-year-olds make language errors. We're there principally to protect their safety and to applaud their successes because we realize that crawling leads to toddling, walking, running, and jumping—and babbling eventually leads to smooth speaking, reading, and writing. It's developmental speed-up time, but we're typically in no hurry. When the neuronal systems that regulate a skill come on line, children spontaneously and joyfully practice the skill. Infants will allow adults to carry them at 3 months but not at 13 months. They appropriately insist on walking, even if they don't do it effectively, since they seem to intuitively know that the only way they will learn to walk is by practicing walking.

At about 5 years, we say in effect, "You can do it with kin; let's now try it with nonkin," and we send them off to school where the developmental tasks and the social setting are more complex. Children tend to closely observe and mimic the social behavior of their parents and other adults, but they're now in a classroom in which they aren't related to anyone, and almost everyone is their own age.

The development of social skills in school thus poses a new and stimulating challenge. Classroom society fortunately provides them with a marvelous laboratory for social learning and exploration—from structured magic circles to free-flowing recess behavior. Their fellow explorers are peers from families espousing a variety of values, and they all have to learn how to get along in an institutional setting that differs considerably from the informality of home. Student misbehavior and disagreements can thus become an important diagnostic part of the social curriculum (much as pain is the first step to physical healing).

The school social environment should be challenging but not too threatening to children who are learning how to negotiate their way through the real nonkin social problems they confront. It certainly helps if the family and neighborhood also enhance a student's personal and social development, but schools must work with whomever comes through the door, at whatever their developmental level, with whatever problems they have. The goal is to help move children to an almost automatic expression of basic social skills (such as occurs with their basic math and language skills).

Language includes the automatic mastery of a verbal taxonomy of generally accepted object, action, quality, and relationship categories. Similarly, morality, ethics, and democratic skills include the mastery of a social taxonomy of culturally acceptable behaviors as the child attempts to satisfy both personal and group needs. A collaborative classroom management model obviously enhances such development.

Our current obsession with raising *academic* standards (focused on veridical knowledge) has led to a diminished focus on school time devoted to the basics of personal and social development and conflict resolution, as well as to a reduction in specialized staff trained to identify and counsel those with a potential for destructive and other forms of antisocial behavior. The recent series of secondary school classmate killings argues for a reexamination of such decisions. The movement of the socially inept to deviant social groups often begins during the elementary school years.

The best long-term strategy for reducing antisocial behavior is probably to identify young children who are at risk and to place them into intervention programs that will help them develop the social skills and coping strategies they need. The First Step to Success program, for example, begins in kindergarten (Walker, 1998).

Self-contained classrooms are common in elementary schools, and they provide a better environment than departmentalized schools for exploring time. Bells don't ring with 45-minute regularity, so activities can be stretched out or compressed. Certain activities, such as library, physical education, and lunch, are scheduled schoolwide, but much exploratory flexibility still exists about the scheduling, length, and spacing of activities. For example, what's best first off, and what's best at the end of the day? Should sedentary activities be followed by movement, and should individual activities be followed by group activities? Are Monday and Friday different kinds of days than Tuesday through Thursday? Find out by exploring ideas with your class, collaboratively trying out different ways to schedule the day, and gathering data on what you do.

Adolescence

We all meander into adult life through an adolescent door. Some go through it relatively easily, but most stumble going over the threshold—their erratic (and, alas, often erotic) stumbling being almost a rite of passage. What's odd is that we adults so often seem surprised and even mystified when we observe adolescents confronting the same problems and doing the same foolish and destructive things we did during our own passage. We often romanticize our own adolescence because we survived it but now worry (as our parents worried about us) that our children won't survive. The good news is that most adolescents finally make it through the door into responsible adulthood.

From ages 11 to 20, adolescents focus on learning how to be a *productive, reproductive human being,* planning for a vocation and exploring emotional commitment and sexuality. The early part of this period is incredibly challenging.

We go through seven profound biological changes during our life, and three of these generally occur between ages 11 and 14 (the middle school years)! The seven changes include birth and death; the mid- to late-life lessening of our reproductive, cognitive, and motor capabilities; and the three major early adolescent shifts:

- from childhood to puberty, the onset of our reproductive capabilities;
- from concrete to formal operations, the (Piagetian) maturation of intelligence; and
- from an authoritarian to a consensus morality, the maturation of our personal and social identity.

The timely adolescent maturation of our brain's frontal lobes is central to the success of all three developmental shifts. The frontal lobes play key roles in attention, adaptive and reflective thought, and problem solving. Highly interconnected with our subcortical, more reflexive processing systems, they can inhibit impulsive and inappropriate behavior.

One could ask how prepuberty children function without mature frontal lobes, and the answer is that they hang around adults who have mature frontal lobes. For all practical purposes, their parents, teachers, and other adults are their frontal lobes—telling them what to do and when to do it, what to eat and what to wear. They don't object too much, just as a 3-month infant doesn't object to being carried. But just as a toddler doesn't want to be carried, so early adolescents no longer appreciate the *frontal lobe-type* advice of their parents. The only way one can learn how to walk is to walk, and the only way to learn how to make decisions is to practice making decisions (such as those that occur in a collaborative classroom).

We could thus consider the years from ages 11 through 20 as a second childhood—the awkward beginnings in each of the three major areas of change, the gradual movement toward the confidence and competence characterized by upper adolescent frontal lobe–driven response patterns that are often delayed and reflective (rather than rapid and reflexive).

Busy as adolescents often are, their life actually slows down somewhat. They hang out, often not doing much of anything. They daydream. Music becomes central to their lives because song slows down what would otherwise be speech and inserts melody, harmony, rhythm, and volume into the long but simple musically emotional messages of love and hate, of commitment and alienation that we use to slowly explore our emerging personal and social relationships. The music of our adolescence helps to define our personal and social identity, even though adults have seemingly always tended to scorn the music their children create and embrace (my parents thought that Glenn Miller's music was sensuously destructive).

Unfortunately, adults frequently don't offer early adolescents the same warm indulgence and social protection that they provided a decade earlier. We appreciated their preadolescent move toward rapid, reflexive, correct responses, and so we now want them to quickly get their act together (oblivious of the reality that many 40-year-olds are still struggling with their sexuality and morality). We respond to the adolescent awkward explorations of sexuality, critical thinking, and identity with a tendency to deride their initial simplistic solutions to complex problems, and we're leery of their early romantic friendships and shifts from our family's values.

Adolescents sense this and typically attempt to distance themselves from the adults who offered them such unconditional nurturing a decade earlier. Adolescents tend to affect clothing, adornment, and behavior styles they know will displease adults. They spend a lot of time in introspection, and they now seek the advice and nurturing that their parents provided earlier from their peers—and, alas, from trashy mass media examples of aggressively inept conflict resolution and romanticism.

Those who didn't develop effective social skills during their first decade must now seek friendships from within a smaller pool of peers, generally those who are similarly rejected by the socially successful. The socially competent will generally support each other since we're a cooperative social species. But we cooperate with those in our perceived group, and we tend to be wary of others, often expressing it in speech and manner. The adolescent alienation of the rejected increases.

Puberty signals the biological capacity for adult relationships and parenthood, and so this parental and family distancing is actually developmentally important. Their adult life will typically be spent more with nonkin than kin, and they can't maintain their primary allegiance to their childhood family while simultaneously beginning the extended process of forming and negotiating their own mature relationships. For example, spousal relationships tend to diminish if one partner is too psychologically tied to his or her childhood family and/or friends.

Unfortunately, our biological readiness for parenthood occurs a decade or so before most adolescents are culturally ready for such commitment. Many thus disassociate from their family in their search for a personal identity, with no bonding alternative in sight. Adolescent organizations and informal social groupings fill the void for many and provide a useful vehicle for developing and rehearsing positive social skills. In a secondary school culture of cliques, however, the socially rejected become even more alienated from peers who could possibly help them if any positive connection could develop. Such negative alliances as troubled couples and adolescent gangs are one unfortunate (but psychologically understandable) solution to this alienation.

The adolescent need to explore their emerging frontal lobe capabilities creates a problem. If a toddler falls down while learning to walk, the damage is usually minor. Conversely, the awkwardness or bad decision of an adolescent can lead to something far more serious—an auto accident, a pregnancy. Self-centered impulsive children must mature into reflective adults who consider the social impact of their decisions and behavior. Unfortunately, the transition is often bumpy; the possibility of trying something exciting is immediately more compelling than their ability to consider potential problems.

Maturity thus often shifts our perspective of what's appropriate behavior. An acquaintance told me that he had gone to a lot of effort and expense to enclose part of his backyard with a beautiful stained wooden fence. The morning following its completion, he discovered that someone—he assumed an adolescent—had used an aerosol paint can during the night to tag the length of the fence with crude words and designs. He was furious. And then he recalled that he and a friend had done something similar to someone's fence when they were 16 and thought it a funny prank. I expect that today's adolescent computer hackers will similarly resent it when future adolescents electronically disable their personal and business records.

An adolescent with immature frontal lobes can thus be sufficiently mature to design and carry out a complex action but not really realize until perhaps years later that the action was very immature and inappropriate. Knowing how to do something isn't the same as knowing if you should do it. The development of a personal moral/ethical base is a central issue in adolescent maturation. A collaborative classroom management model gives young people many opportunities to make decisions and observe and learn from the results of their decisions. The secondary school extracurricular program also provides many excellent opportunities for adolescents to make decisions in areas that interest them (such as the school paper, planning a dance, and sports team activity).

Secondary schools tend to be departmentalized and often seem more concerned with the successful mastery of subjects than with the social maturation of adolescents. Since secondary schools are typically more beset by political pressures to excel, they're more oriented toward increasing the pressure on students during a decade in which adolescents need to slow down, consolidate the explosive motor and social development of their first decade, and so discover themselves. Elementary school class explorations of how best to understand and use class time seem an impossible luxury to secondary school teachers, and yet it's equally necessary to explore adolescent time.

For example, at puberty, many young people go through a period of continual jet lag. They seem now to live a couple time zones west from where they actually are, going to bed and awakening later than formerly. It's related to the hormonal changes young people go through at puberty. We've always known about it (even if we didn't understand it), but the secondary school buses and school schedule run as if all adolescents are wide awake by 8 a.m. The result, as any secondary school teacher knows, is that the first periods are a drowsy disaster for many students. Any hope for a creative solution?

Perhaps. We're approaching a time when schools will have much more access to computer technology. The secondary school curriculum is composed of elements that are (1) personally directed and can thus be processed and mastered individually through computer software or (2) best mastered through the social interaction of students in a classroom.

One could therefore imagine a future secondary school schedule that would focus on individual computer-driven studies from (perhaps) 8 to 10 a.m. and 3 to 5 p.m. and socially interactive curricula from 10 a.m. to 3 p.m. Students would attend from 8 a.m. to 3 p.m. or from 10 a.m. to 5 p.m. (depending on their sleep/waking cycle or other commitments). The school would need enough individual computer technology for half the student body in the early and late segments and enough classroom space to accommodate all students during the midday block when all are present. Existing schools typically have that spatial capability. Staff schedules could be shifted to accommodate the longer day so that students would have at least periodic individual access to their teachers (as needed) during the individually oriented blocks at the beginning and end of the day.

It's not an impossible scenario, despite all sorts of problems with bus schedules, sports, teacher schedules, staff meetings, the availability of useful software, and whatever other problems folks will suggest. But nothing will ever change unless educators begin to imagine that there might be a better way to organize time in an adolescent student's life and then seek creative solutions.

A YEAR'S CURRICULAR TIME

We can separate the division of time in both our personal lives and the school curriculum into three categories of activity that are driven by internal and external forces.

1. Some of our lifetime is prescribed by societal needs, such as to be a productive citizen, and so our job demands our attendance during certain time blocks.

2. Some of our time is prescribed by human conditions, such as to care for our own bodily needs and to come to the aid of an injured person.

3. Some of our time is devoted to personal interests, such as hobbies, mass media, and recreation.

We differ much in our allocation of time to these three categories. Some people must work long hours at a low-paying job to merely survive, and so personal needs and interests get limited time. Others are retired or independently wealthy, and so they may spend most of their time on such things as personal interests, body care, and charitable endeavors.

A school year has about 1,000 hours. We can divide curricular time into the same three categories and raise the issue of the appropriate time allocation among the three.

The Formal Curriculum

Most people consider the term *curriculum* to be related to such concepts as the required courses and programs, scope and sequence issues, and state standards. The formal curriculum represents society's concern for prescribed minimum mastery standards in selected socially important subject areas and the belief that instruction should proceed in a systematic fashion. Most of the instructional and materials budget is spent on this part of the curriculum.

The language arts, in their various forms, dominate this part of the elementary curriculum. Furthermore, vocabulary development (learning the names of things) is a major focus of most other elementary curricular areas such as science and social studies. The secondary school curriculum is a mix of required and elective courses, with the total number and focus of academic units being what is formally prescribed. Large schools tend to have a richer assortment of elective courses.

The formal curriculum is important in that it develops standardization and balance in a school system in which students transfer among schools. But it can become a negative force if it so dominates the program that educators and patrons ignore other important elements in the education of young people. The negative human-time equivalent of this limited perspective would be workaholics, who are so psychologically tied to the perceived demands of their job that they don't know what to do and can't relax at home, on vacations, and upon retirement.

The Responsive Curriculum

This part of the curriculum focuses on (often-unpredictable) events that intrude into the curriculum because of their immediate noteworthiness—a war, a disaster, a community celebration, a house being moved down the street, or a death. The social significance of this phenomenon is underscored by an immense journalistic enterprise that uses print and electronic technology to inform us about what occurred elsewhere. These local and media-reported events are prescribed in that it's almost impossible to ignore them, even though they might not easily fit into the current curriculum. In nonschool terms, it's like a car accident intruding on an already busy day. One simply has to reschedule things and respond to the importance and immediacy of the accident.

Curricular guides and materials for unpredictable developments are typically nonexistent. Teachers tend to create something on the fly as the events unfold. I was a sixth-grade teacher on Saturday,

October 5, 1957, when the world's first satellite (*Sputnik*) went into orbit. The Russians had made no previous announcement of their intentions.

I realized when the event was reported on the evening news that it would become a major historical event in my students' lives, and so I decided to focus on it on Monday, despite my general lack of knowledge of the topic. I went to the library to learn as much as possible, and I checked the district's AV catalog for any useful materials. I (and many other teachers, I'm sure) initiated a study of rockets and satellites on Monday. I told my students that we would have to be co-learners in the enterprise since my knowledge was limited. They were delighted to discover an important topic that they knew as much about as their teacher (practically nothing), and so we collaborated on designing an investigation that went on for several weeks (and intruded seriously into the formal curriculum). We ended our study by making and launching rockets.

Many classes make and launch rockets now, but it's much more exciting to do something like this at the point of the historical event. I've chanced upon several students in that class over the years, and most told me without prompting that our satellite study was the most memorable event of their elementary school years.

The assassinations of President Kennedy and Martin Luther King, Jr., the *Challenger* explosion (observed on classroom TV by many students because a teacher was aboard), the eruption of Mt. St. Helens, the Clinton impeachment trial, the recent series of high school murders, and the World Trade Center destruction are other examples of major unpredictable historical events that teachers had to respond to at one level or another.

Teachers sometimes know about an important coming event that doesn't easily fit into the current formal curriculum—such as a presidential election, a community centennial celebration, or the first moon landing—and can prepare for it. Mass media and the Internet are generally a rich source of information for such curricular investigations.

Certain classes of events are unpredictable but have a high probability of occurring during the course of the year, and so teachers often determine in advance how they will handle such situations should they occur. A death, storm damage, and the closing of a company that employs the parents of many students are examples.

One problem with this part of the curriculum is that teachers get limited guidance for how to deal with such problem situations, and the immediacy of the event can lead to an inappropriate response. A university student told me that her father died in an accident when she was in the fourth grade, and so she missed a week of school. Her teacher asked her classmates before her return to avoid comments and questions about the death—the less said the better. A dozen years later, she was still deeply grieved that her father had lived a loving and productive life, and when he died, neither his life nor his death were mentioned in her classroom by a teacher and classmates who, she now realizes, incorrectly thought they were being kind to her.

The Informal Curriculum

This segment of the curriculum focuses on cultural areas of special interest to teachers and/or students. They arise out of avocations, hobbies, the nature of the class, the availability of materials, and the location of the school. They are neither required nor prohibited by the school. They get into the curriculum because people enjoy doing them, and so they add a pinch of spice to the curriculum. I've known many teachers who insert their personal interests and hobbies into the curriculum.

I was interested in the Japanese art of origami (paper folding), and so I always taught it to my elementary school students. No one said I should, and no one said I shouldn't. My students enjoyed it in part because they discovered a little bit of me and my interests in the process—and origami is an intriguing challenge.

Conversely, a fifth-grade teacher I once met had an extensive mineral collection and knew a lot about geology. When I asked him how he incorporated his knowledge and collection into his teaching, he told me that he didn't mention it to his students, let alone teach it. He said that in his previous school, students were always bringing rocks to him to identify. It finally irritated him, and so he decided to keep his hobby to himself at his current school. How absolutely sad!

Every class has students with knowledge that should be tapped. Years later, I can still recall a budding fourth-grade ornithologist who did most of the teaching in our science unit on birds, a fifth grader who proudly took us on a field trip through his parents' paint business, a sixth grader who taught us how to compose songs, and a seventh grader who taught us all to weave. This informal part of the curriculum gets to the heart of primary grade show-and-tell time, elementary school interest groups, and secondary school electives and extracurricular programs.

I've always found the discussion interesting when a group of educators tries to determine how time should properly be apportioned among these three categories of curricular time. Ask a group of teachers to individually jot down percentages that indicate approximately (1) how much time they currently devote to each category across the year and then (2) how they would prefer to allocate the 100% among the three categories. Tabulate and graph the results. What factors might affect the allocations—grade level, years of experience, gender? It's interesting for teachers to hear their colleagues explain their allocations and the differences between their practice and preference.

Informal surveys discovered that inexperienced teachers tended to focus on the formal curriculum. This isn't surprising since they are concerned with their continued employment and so realize they must do well with district programs that they are still trying to understand. We also found that teachers with many years of experience who seemed to be suffering from burnout focused more on the formal curriculum, and this also isn't surprising. It's what a veteran teacher can typically teach with the least effort.

Teachers who seemed an imaginative cut above the norm tended to focus more on the responsive curriculum. Their comments suggested that they were aware of educationally significant events that occurred in the community and beyond, and they inserted such events into the curriculum, often finding ways to insert these events into the formal curriculum or to encourage interested students to explore them through informal investigations.

This time allocation is also a good issue for an elementary or secondary class to explore. Introduce the issue by asking them to keep a log for several days indicating how they apportioned their personal time across the three categories (societal demands, body needs, and personal interests). Then keep records on how class time was allocated across the categories for a couple weeks. The study should lead to discussions and explorations of different curricular time allocations.

A Day in the Life

We live through about 150,000 hours between the ages of 1 and 18. We sleep about 50,000 hours of this time, partly because dwindling stores of glycogen in our awake active brain induce sleep, during which glycogen is replenished. Glycogen is a complex carbohydrate that provides short-term energy storage for brain and muscle tissue (Cobb, 2002).

We dream about 2 hours of the 8 hours we sleep each night, and sleeping and dreaming appear to be positively related to the development and maintenance of the long-term memories that emerge out of daytime activities because they allow our brain to eliminate the interference of sensorimotor activity while it physically adds to, edits, and erases the neural network connections that create long-term memories.

We spend about 65,000 of our 100,000 waking hours involved in solitary activities and in direct, informal value-laden relationships with family and friends, activities that play a major role in the development and maintenance of important *personal* memories and interests.

We spend about 35,000 of our waking hours with our larger culture in formal and informal metaphoric-symbolic activities—about 12,000 hours in school and about twice that much with the various forms of mass media (such as TV, computers, films, music, sports, nonschool print media, churches, and museums). Mass media and the school thus play major roles in the development and maintenance of important *cultural* memories and skills.

So on an average developmental day between the ages of 1 and 18, a young person sleeps 8 hours; spends 10 waking hours with self, family, and friends; spends 4 hours with mass media; and spends only 2 hours in school. Our society has incredible expectations for those 2 hours!

We can think of the family as a vertically organized social system composed of people of various ages who live together. The parental older members typically control the resources, and they do what they can to inculcate their values into the younger members. Parents are thus much interested in promoting their personal view of the concepts of right and wrong.

A K–12 classroom is a horizontally organized social system composed of a group of young people of about the same age (and one older official representative of adult society). The students come from separate (vertically organized) families that may differ substantially in their values on many issues. As indicated in Chapter 3, schools thus focus mostly on the less controversial concepts of true and false—veridical (factual) information and skills with high community agreement (such as that $6 \times 5 = 30$, c-a-t spells *cat,* and

Washington, D.C. is the capital of the United States). Schools have historically avoided controversial (right/wrong) cultural issues, such as issues related to religious beliefs, sexual practices, and politics. Schools may explain the expressed (true/false) differences among political parties on a given issue but will not presume to indicate which position is right or wrong.

It's actually difficult to identify any cultural value that enjoys total community agreement. Even the seemingly straightforward injunction to not kill people is fraught with disagreement when one considers such value-laden cultural practices as abortion, capital punishment, war, mercy killing, industrial pollution, and assisted suicide.

Classroom management policies and practices obviously involve value judgments, from attention to bad manners, crude language, dress, and beyond. But it's one thing to create school behavioral boundaries and another thing to say (for example) that certain expressions are inherently crude (when a student's parents may commonly use the terms at home). Almost everything that occurs in school is value laden (and so adaptive) at one level or another, but educators try to distinguish between a value decision the school made to maintain order and the absolute *rightness* of that decision. Classroom management thus involves a lot of negotiating among educators, students, and parents. Chapter 8 will revisit this issue.

Behavioral evaluation is a difficult issue. Public schools must initially accept the values of entering students and their families (assuming that their values aren't illegal), even though the student's behavior may be somewhat troublesome. The school begins where the students are and works toward eventual student acceptance of school behavioral expectations. It's curious that parents, who are often so insistent about periodic precise evaluations of their children's school development, do not grade their home behavior, even though they have much more personal access to their children's behavior than the school. The reason is perhaps that family values generally develop through an extended period of negotiation between parents and child, and it's difficult for parents to assess the strength of the family values at any given time. (One could argue that it's equally difficult to precisely assess much of the veridical/adaptive school learning that parents expect educators to precisely assess.)

It's important to realize that many agencies other than the family and school play key enculturation roles during childhood and adolescence. Electronic mass media have especially emerged recently to considerably broaden children's access to the world. What occurs anywhere is now known everywhere. Mass media provide a curious mix of information and values. The credibility of the information varies tremendously, and impressionable young people often lack the ability to differentiate sense from nonsense in mass media.

Although the family controls (or ought to control) a child's access to these other enculturation agencies, students typically bring a wide range of information and values from such agencies into a classroom's curriculum. Even though the school has no control over the information children gather during nonschool time, parents may become distressed that such information got inserted into a class discussion.

Chapter 4 posed the issue of the appropriate control of a classroom year. It suggested that one could metaphorically think of (1) an externally controlled, protected environment (akin to that of a fetus in a womb) in which the school would control curricular content and events or (2) a more self-controlled, exploratory environment (akin to that of a person's life), quite open to the extended collaborative exploration of a wide range of information and values.

Although school actually occupies a relatively small part of a child's first two decades, it does get prime time, and the students generally don't have a remote control to change the channel if they don't like the current curriculum (as they do with mass media and other nonschool activities). School time is thus important time in a student's life, even though its focus generally differs from personal, family, peer, and mass media time. School provides access to information and skills that are rarely the focus of these other educative agencies. It's organized to enhance social awareness and skills. It often moves a student beyond immediate family values and traditions into contacts with other ways of thinking about and doing things.

This chapter began with the suggestion that our culture tends to think of time as a commodity, and so a continuing challenge to educators is to spend school time wisely, despite a lack of clear consensus on how that might be done.

Suggested Activities

Students tend to experience each school day for what it is and to not notice the gradual sweep of time over the school year. The following activities provide them with a sense of that.

A Room Diary

This yearlong activity works best in an elementary self-contained classroom or middle school homeroom. Schedule the students so that one student is assigned each day to be the room reporter (and to not participate directly in class activities and assignments). Locate the reporter at a separate table with a good view of the entire room (to facilitate the observation and recording of formal and informal events). It's also a good idea to ask the student to take one picture (on a digital camera) of the event that best photographically characterized the day. Toward the end of the day, ask the student to summarize his or her observations into a one-page narrative report of what occurred that was interesting and memorable and to read it to the class just before dismissal.

Ask the student to type the report into a word processor form (that allows space to insert the picture onto the page, if you include a photograph in this diary activity). It's also useful to include such information as attendance and weather into each day's report. Print a copy of the day's report and place it into a three-ring binder.

The next person on the list becomes the reporter the next day. Over the course of the year, each student will be the reporter about six times. Students will read the diary frequently during the year, and it will become a useful reference about events and decisions. It's obviously important at the beginning of the year to instruct them in how to observe, record, and summarize a day and to caution them against hurtful comments (humor is great, ridicule isn't).

The marvelous thing about this activity is that at the end of the year, you can duplicate a copy of the room diary (perhaps 180 pages) for each student. Teach a bookbinding unit toward the end of the year, and each student will leave with a complete, personally bound record of the year. If the duplicating/binding cost per diary (under $5) creates a problem, encourage your class to explore creative fundraising activities.

A Headline Diary

Cut out the lead-page headline of the local paper each day of the school year and, starting at the top, paste the headlines in sequence on a sheet of butcher paper. Newspaper pages are usually about a foot wide, and the lead headline is about an inch high. It would thus require about a 3-foot-by-1-foot sheet of paper to record the major event of each day during a month. Discuss the events that they most remember at the end of each month. At the end of the year, post and discuss the entire set of headlines.

If your community has several TV stations, it's interesting to report, compare, and discuss the lead story in each station's early evening news (and also on the network news).

A Vine Line

Use a fast-growing vine (such as ivy) to record important events across the year. Plant it into a pot in one corner of the room, continually remove lateral growth, train it up the wall so it's above the chalkboard, and then allow it to grow horizontally along the top of the chalkboard and beyond, as far around the room as it can move over the course of the year.

Attach identifying index cards to the wall, and place an arrow at the point where the tip of the vine is on specific days during the year (such as Halloween, students' birthdays). It's also fun for students to predict (a month or so in advance) where the vine tip might be on their birthday.

Birthdays

About a week or so before their birthdays, ask students to go to the school and public libraries and use newspapers and magazines to discover what important events occurred in the community and world on the day they were born (or shortly before and after). Their parents and other relatives may also be able to provide such information (although some parents are so concerned with the birth that the rest of the world doesn't really register that day). Ask students to report their discoveries on the school day closest to their birthday. They might also want to report the most interesting event in their lives or in the world since their last birthday. It's important for your students to begin to develop a sense of the relationship between their lifetime and world history.

On a personal note, I've always been fascinated that Charles Lindbergh flew across the Atlantic 3 months after I was born, that DNA was discovered 4 years after I graduated from college with a degree in biology, and that the computer chip was developed shortly before I joined the University of Oregon faculty. Thus, commercial flight developed during my lifetime, biology and medicine matured tremendously during my professional life, and the computer revolution occurred during my last job!

Wait Time

Wait time is the amount of time that teachers will wait after asking a question before they ask another student or answer it themselves. It actually averages around 3 seconds, and the better students usually get more time to respond than the poorer students. You can check yourself by giving a student a stopwatch and asking him or her to record your behavior during a lesson—the length of the series of intervals between a question you ask and when you speak again if no student response is forthcoming. You may discover that although we seek reflective thought in the classroom, we often encourage a reflexive rhythm.

CHAPTER SEVEN

Collaboratively Managing Biological and Cultural Movement

Movement is a manifestation of life itself. Even in seeming stillness, our body teems with movement—the beat of our heart, the contractions and expansions of our lungs, the movement of digesting food, neural impulses coursing through our brain, and viral and bacterial invaders moving about. To be perfectly still is to be perfectly dead.

Chapter 2 suggested that the central reason we have a brain is to regulate our own movements and to predict the movements of others and of objects. Plants seem to do fine without a brain, with many trees far outliving us. We have a brain because we have leg, arm, and head muscle systems that allow us to move toward opportunities and away from danger. Plants must stay and take whatever comes along, including predators that nibble leaves and commit other indignities (toxins and bark providing limited protection, as suggested in Chapter 5). Why would an immobile tree even want a sensory system that could recognize an approaching logger?

Consider the sea squirt, an organism that initially has a brain and swims about until it finds a place with sufficient nutrients. It then permanently attaches to a nearby rock or coral and begins the rest of its immobile life by eating its now superfluous brain.

Since we humans move throughout life, we need an intelligent cognitive system that can transform sensory input and imagination into appropriate motor output—to decide what's good and bad about here and there and then to move or stay. Mobility is thus central to much that's human, whether the movement of information is physical or psychological (such as running toward or speaking to someone). We can move and talk. Trees can't. Misguided teachers who constantly tell their students to sit down and be quiet imply a preference for working with a grove of trees rather than a classroom of mobile articulate students.

We can think of ourselves as inside-out crustaceans. A crustacean's skeleton is on the outside; ours is on the inside. Our soft tissue and appendages are out where we can readily observe them.

Having an internal skeleton means that we have a direct intimate, sensory knowledge of how our external motor system functions. From birth on, we can observe and feel muscular contractions and their relationship to body movements. We've also created tools that accurately measure the properties of our marvelous movement system. Furthermore, we've always celebrated this basic universal understanding and awe of our motor system through performance and competitions.

It's intriguing that we've developed a simple common human understanding of movement through our continuous observation of its dynamics, but we lack that direct understanding about our cognitive processes (which are more crustacean-like, hidden within a bony skull and spinal cord). For example, we can't hear the sounds active neurons make, or smell our brain, or sense the movement of neurotransmitters—and our brain itself has no pain receptors (although it registers pain occurring elsewhere).

This lack of direct sensory access to our cognitive processes led to the development of many competing speculations and theories about how our brain/mind functions. Indeed, Behaviorism, which dominated psychology for much of this past century, focused on the observable motor behavior that emerges out of cognition rather than on cognitive activity, which then was inaccessible. As indicated in Chapter 2, brain imaging technology is now providing an analogous direct observational window into our active cognitive functions that we've always enjoyed with our movement functions.

This book focuses principally on energy, space, time, movement, and range as they relate to the management of life and classrooms.

When we expend *energy* in our *space/time* world, *movement* within biological and cultural *ranges* generally occurs. Movement thus combines energy, space, and time within limits.

It's also probably safe to say that most classroom misbehavior involves the movement of people, objects, or sounds—running, slouching, hitting, throwing things, being noisy, using vulgar language, and so on. Many disciplinary measures also involve movement (or nonmovement), such as a verbal reprimand, movement toward the misbehaving student, a request to sit down, an office referral, or detention.

This chapter will thus explore several important elements of physical and psychological movement that relate to classroom management:

PHYSICAL MOVEMENT

Motor Development and Maintenance

Although a cognitive decision to move may involve many millions of neurons, only about a half million motor neurons are involved in activating the muscle groups that make up almost half of our body weight. Our jointed motor system with its complex brain and muscle connections provides our brain with a remarkably effective external mechanism for action. It's composed of the toe, foot, and leg system that's about half our body's length; the finger, hand, and arm system that extends our reach about 2 feet beyond our body; a flexible neck that increases the geographic range of our head's sensory receptors; and a remarkable mouth that begins digestion and also communicates through both sound and expressive facial movements.

Several brain systems (notably the basal ganglia, parietal lobes, motor cortex, and cerebellum) coordinate the actual initiation and execution of movement, acting as a sort of virtual reality center that initially simulates projected movements to accelerate and better control our actual movements. This neuronal system constantly draws on internal models, automatic programs, and sensory feedback to analyze our current body position and movement goals as it predicts and then activates the appropriate motor commands. It's amazing how well the system predicts such things as the weight of the object, the height of the stair step, or the distance to the target before sending out motor commands, and it's generally processing several major motor commands simultaneously! It's an excellent system, but not perfect. If it were, professional basketball players would always shoot free throws successfully, we'd never spill soup on our clothing, and life would indeed be boring.

Not surprisingly, our sensitive sensory system and finely controlled movements are central to the visual, aural, and movement arts (including most sports, which are basically a dance form). The arts play an important role in our culture because (among other values) they provide a stimulating and often pleasant means for developing and maintaining our motor system up to virtuoso levels. Consider the fine motor control of a painter, the practiced pizzicato of a violinist, or the choreographed pick-and-roll of an NBA team. Since movement is so central to being human, we really ought to do it with style and grace, and the arts do enhance the development and maintenance of both choreographed and improvised movements.

Chapter 6 suggested that the development of a smoothly controlled motor system is a major childhood priority. Suckling is almost the first mobile act of an infant, followed by the brain-outward maturation of the arm and leg systems—eating before grasping before walking. Since mobility is a central human characteristic, these innate systems must develop early at the survival level without formal instruction. This motor development includes specific currently ill-understood periods during which various key specialized brain systems generally develop (such as walking at about age 1, talking at about age 2).

How infants begin their mastery of complex motor behaviors is a fascinating developmental phenomenon. Consider a behavior that most parents observe. If you stick out your tongue to an observant infant shortly after birth, the probability is high that the infant will reciprocate the behavior.

Sticking out our tongue is an uncommon act for humans, and it requires the activation of a complex motor neuron sequence. Our tongue is a very important muscle that is used to facilitate eating and speech, so we normally keep it inside our mouth. I suppose it would be possible for an infant to randomly fire the appropriate motor neurons for tongue projection, but that's not what occurs when an infant sticks out her tongue in immediate mimicry of a parent's action. How can an infant possibly master such a complex motor act immediately after observing it?

Scientists have discovered a remarkable system they call *mirror neurons* that explains the modeling and mimicking process that is central to much human learning. Their initial studies involved a left-hemisphere area called Broca's area that regulates speech production. In a presentation at Cambridge University that was posted on the Internet, renowned neuroscientist V. S. Ramachandran (2000) suggested that the discovery of mirror neurons might provide the same powerful unifying framework for our understanding of teaching and learning that the discovery of DNA did for our understanding of genetics.

A smoothly coordinated motor sequence involves the typically unconscious preparation for a movement followed by the actual movement. For example, while my left index finger is typing the *c* in *cat,* my left little finger is getting ready to type *a* and my left index finger will shortly move up to the top row to type the *t.* The result is a single seamless typing action—*cat.*

Chapter 5 reported that the motor cortex plays a key role in activating such muscles. It's a narrow ear-to-ear band of neural tissue, with specific segments dedicated to regulating specific groups of body muscles. The premotor area directly in front of the motor cortex primes the next movements in a motor sequence.

Scientists have recently discovered that neurons in the premotor area that fire in preparation for upcoming movements also fire when we observe someone else carry out that action (Meltzoff & Prinz, 2002). Common brain regions thus process both the perception and production of a movement. The infant's observation of her parent's projecting tongue fires the premotor neurons that represent her tongue, and this priming activates the related motor cortex neurons that project her tongue out in mimicry.

We experience this mimicking phenomenon most commonly when we see someone yawn, and then typically we have to stifle our own yawn. Since infants must learn many movements, they don't inhibit the mimicking of movements they observe. For them, it's *monkey see, monkey do* (and it's interesting that the initial mirror neuron research was done on monkeys).

Our mirror neurons won't fire at the mere observation of a hand or mouth—only when it's carrying out a goal-directed action. Furthermore, they will respond to a hand but not a tool that's grasping or moving an object (since body parts and not tools are represented in our motor and premotor areas).

Mirror neurons may thus facilitate the preliminary motor neuron simulation, priming, programming, and rehearsing that occur in children, and this process obviously enhances our eventual mastery of complex motor behaviors and our ability to *read* the minds of others. For example, inferring the potential movements of others is an essential skill in many games in which players try to *fake out* opponents. Mirror neuron stimulation may also explain why so many people enjoy observing the movements of virtuoso athletes, dancers, and musicians. It allows us to mentally represent actions we can't physically mimic. Note the related active body language of former athletes as they observe a game they once played.

Scientists are also exploring the relationship between mirror neuron activity and our ability to imagine our own planned actions, be empathetic, and develop articulate speech. Mirror neurons may thus eventually help to explain many teaching and learning mysteries in which modeling provides children with an effective behavioral pattern to follow, as well as explain disabilities (such as autism) in which children can't *read* the minds of others.

Children denied the opportunity to observe and thus develop a motor-driven survival skill that they would normally master with ease during its preferred developmental period may not recover from the deprivation. A good example is the tragic case of Genie, who was 13 when discovered hidden naked in a closet. Her mentally disturbed parents had almost totally deprived her of normal language and motor development. Competent therapists who then tried to undo the damage were only marginally successful (Rymer, 1993).

Since children tend to imitate the actions of others, it's important to teach them to be discriminating—to imitate appropriate behavior and to suppress any tendency to imitate inappropriate behavior. Cooperative learning activities and a collaborative classroom provide many opportunities to observe and evaluate behavior.

Most folks realize that the cognitive and motor systems that process language must be stimulated early and regularly to master the local spoken and written language, and we correctly insist that schools focus on the key elements. But communicative motor development certainly involves more than that. For example, within the same student brain is another set of neural systems that process musical forms that are distinct from articulate speech. Song uses such elements as tone, melody, harmony, and rhythm to insert important emotional overtones into a now slowed-down verbal message. Our brain's language and (verbal/nonverbal) music systems must both be developmentally stimulated, especially those subsystems that regulate highly controlled motor activity (such as speaking and singing, writing, and musical instrument playing).

Both communicative forms permeate our culture (and Chapter 6 suggested that music plays an especially important role during adolescence). How can anyone justify a curriculum that seeks to develop language but not musical capabilities? Is spelling really *biologically* more important than melody when both express culturally significant sequential information?

Are our innate music networks (and other educationally ignored cognitive/motor systems) something like unwanted tonsils or appendix tissue to be removed rather than understood and enhanced? It's difficult to imagine how anyone involved with educational policy can have such a limited view of our brain and the curriculum. Recall the plight of Genie discussed above. How many musically limited students are now emerging from school, having had practically no competent professional development of their innate musical ability or, for that matter, of their spatial processing centers that are so central to the visual and movement arts? How foolish we've been in recent years to eliminate trained teachers and programs especially tuned to such developmentally important systems.

We're born into a very complex world with an immature brain, one-third its adult size. Since we can live in a wide variety of environments, our sensory/motor development beyond innate survival needs tends to focus on the specific environmental demands that each brain confronts. Highly specialized and coordinated movement patterns, such as those used in calligraphy, playing the violin, and tap dancing, must thus be taught, and mastery is typically difficult. The importance of the early acquisition of such skills was demonstrated in a recent study of right-handed violinists (Elbert et al., 1995). Separate, specific motor cortex areas control right- and left-hand finger movements. Violinists who began lessons before the age of 12 developed important strengths in the size and complexity of these motor areas that didn't develop in nonviolinists (who had less need for the left-hand digital dexterity required in right-handed violinists) or even in good violinists who began later.

Michael Jordan, a recent basketball superstar, is another interesting example (Klawans, 1996). At age 31, he decided to fulfill a dream and switch to baseball. With all of his athletic ability and resolve, he didn't do nearly as well as he had hoped. Throwing a basketball through a hoop requires different sensory and motor skills than hitting a 90+-mph baseball. Even major league pitchers are not recycled into hitters when their pitching abilities wane, although they understand the game and batted during the games they pitched.

Survival-level cognitive and motor skills are universal and innate. Explicit early instruction and effort can get us beyond mere survival levels into the normal limits of human capability. Virtuoso-level abilities are highly specific and require the commitment of early extensive training. Many young people exhibit this skill-specific commitment when they continuously practice specialized skills. Call it play if you will, but Jean Piaget suggested that play is the serious business of childhood.

Collaborative classroom activities should provide many opportunities for the development of all educationally relevant motor skills beyond mere survival. Chapter 4 reported the research that indicated that elevated levels of the neurotransmitter serotonin enhance relaxation and the calm assurance that leads to smoothly controlled and coordinated movement patterns, and such movements tend to increase one's self-esteem. Too many classrooms continue to be a pencil-driven sedentary environment that's quite removed from the complex mobility that human biology seeks and now desperately needs in an era increasingly influenced by movement technologies (such as the peculiar phenomenon of parents driving their children a short distance to soccer practice). It's true that students spend most of their life in nonschool settings that often encourage biological mobility, but do work with your students to create a more biologically mobile classroom.

Sound as Movement

Sound (the result of information-laden rhythmically moving air molecules reaching eardrums) is perhaps the most common form of classroom movement. Given the size and composition of the group, classrooms tend to be relatively quiet, and teachers are expected to keep them that way. A quiet classroom and a successful language arts program are important factors when evaluating an elementary teacher's performance, despite the apparent contradiction. A considerable body of evidence (and common knowledge) indicates that the teacher typically talks as much or more as all the rest of the class put together, and teachers don't have to ask permission to talk.

Why, then, does classroom noise upset teachers (and it's generally high on teacher annoyance lists)? What else can one reasonably expect from a couple dozen students working together for hours in a room with many sound-reflecting hard, smooth surfaces where communication defines the very experience? Well, why not get upset by classroom noise? The sounds of normal social interaction differ considerably from the noise of distraction that draws attention away from the learning activities that brought the class together.

It's a dilemma. Most educators would be hard-pressed to precisely explain the difference between the sounds of productive classwork and distracting classroom noise, but almost all can easily differentiate between the two in an actual active classroom.

It's often possible to reduce distracting classroom noise by creating buffers that absorb sound within the room (such as strategically placed plants and fabric hangings). Experienced teachers also discover that when they speak softly, it encourages students to be quieter so they can hear better. Model and teach your students how to speak with a 12-inch, 24-inch, or 48-inch voice (the distance at which another person can easily hear comments), and then indicate during different class activities which voice is appropriate (a conversation between two students suggests 12 inches, a comment during a class discussion requires 48 inches).

Desks are typically arranged in the center of the classroom, and this compresses students and so increases distracting sounds. If you have this problem, experiment with arrangements that group desks around the edge of the room. You'll spread out the sound, and create a useful empty space in the middle of the room where (for example) students can assemble in chairs or on the floor in a compact circle for (quieter) discussion activities. Furthermore, you can place sound and visual buffers in the central area to reduce distracting stimuli.

Teachers tend to respond to the almost constant undercurrent of classroom sound with an ongoing string of verbal reprimands ("Quiet down now," "John and Tom, please stop your conversation and get to work," "Walk quietly to the door"). Verbal and nonverbal sounds are thus the most common classroom distraction, and continuing verbal reprimands are the most common management measure. How intriguing!

Frequently used disciplinary measures tend to be ineffective since if they were effective, teachers wouldn't have to continually use them. So why do intelligent, experienced teachers continue to use a management technique of limited effectiveness? A sixth grader explained it beautifully:

Well, most teachers are fair or at least they want to be fair. They know that just asking kids to quiet down doesn't really work, but they do it anyway, because they know a few of the kids will quiet down. Then they raise their voices and holler a little bit, and some more kids quiet down. Then they threaten the noisy ones and some more quiet down. By that time they found out who the really noisy kids are, and they give them serious punishments. Now it wouldn't be fair to punish everyone for being noisy right away, because some kids are just being noisy because that's normal. So the teacher does the things that don't really work on those students to find out who they are, and then only punishes those who didn't quit when she gave them a chance. That's being fair, even if it doesn't work very well.

How eloquent. What the comment suggests is that students have a practical grasp of the inner dynamics of classroom management, and informal studies and simple observation indicate not surprisingly that students who frequently misbehave (and are thus central to the problem) seem to have a better grasp of management dynamics than students identified as well behaved. Since the students' perspective of management differs from the teacher's, they can become useful collaborators on devising procedures for reducing common distractions such as classroom noise. Students consider fairness to be very important in management.

Touch, Where Movement Stops

Touch is probably the most problematic of all the movement-related issues in classroom management. We first learn the difference between others and ourselves through touch, and we continue to explore the positive and negative manifestations of tactile relationships throughout life.

Our brain and skin are the first two organs to emerge in the human embryo, and they develop out of the same layer of embryonic tissue—one side of the layer develops into our 3-pound brain, and the other develops into the 6-pound, 20–square foot mantle of skin that covers our body. We can thus think of our skin as the outside layer of our brain since our sense organs are imbedded in skin. Our skin is the largest organ in our body and the most sensitive to environmental dangers and opportunities because when anything physically bad happens, our skin gets whacked first.

Two separate sets of sensory neurons project information from our skin to our brain. One set carries information about intensive contact and pressure (such as pinching and striking) into the sensory areas of the cortex. The other set carries information about soothing touches (such as caressing and embracing) into the area deep inside our brain that's associated with nurturing, romance, and sexual arousal. Most folks won't be surprised to discover that these nurturing and romantic neurons tend to be located in hairy skin areas (such as our arms, head, and pubic areas), and those associated with more intense touch are located in nonhairy areas (such as palms and the bottom of our feet).

Our brain combines the information from both systems into an integrated emotional sense of our contact with the external world. Perhaps most interesting, the neurons that process nurturing function efficiently from the early hours of life. We're born ready for nurturing caresses.

While verbal reprimands often bounce unheard off student eardrums, physical punishment signals the absolute end of unproductive verbal interaction. Although some folks still promote spanking and other forms of physical punishment as necessary and therapeutic, it's something that rarely occurs now in schools, and it tends to leave everyone dissatisfied. As the sixth grader above implied, the threat of corporal punishment typically works only with those who don't need it. Those whose behavior we wish to improve through corporal punishment tend to shrug it off as part of their continuing "sometimes you win, sometimes you lose" battle with the system.

The discussion earlier in this chapter argued that neural systems that process language, music, and motor systems must be stimulated to reach their potential. Similarly, the gentle holding, hugging, caressing, and nuzzling that most children receive within their extended family during their preschool years helps to activate and mature neural systems that enhance physically close relationships. It's common knowledge now that children who don't receive such loving tactile stimulation suffer from the deprivation. The adolescent years are another such important period when (generally nonfamily) touch and other forms of physical closeness enhance sexual maturation.

But we have a school problem with touching during the entire K–12 span. Many (touch-deprived) students who would benefit much from positive teacher hugs probably won't get them in the current climate because educators are concerned about potential charges of child molestation and sexual harassment and simply don't want to take the risk. It's a sad problem without a simple solution.

Student physical aggression is another problem without a simple solution. So many school and nonschool events can trigger the stress that triggered the shoving or the fight that it's difficult to predict when physical aggression will occur and who will be involved. Since relatively innocuous brushing-to-bumping contacts can quickly escalate into push-back and fighting behaviors if a currently short-tempered student was brushed, it's always wise to organize school movement patterns so that they minimize unwanted physical contact. When a fight begins, the best strategy is to quickly physically separate the fighters until tempers cool and you have an opportunity to discover what caused the problem. Since this is something that will occur periodically during the year, discuss the problem with your students and teach them how to immediately try to talk the fighters into separating if no teacher is readily available to take over. The advantage of creating such a rational strategy is that it raises a typically unconscious action to the level of conscious thought, and this in itself may reduce the number of class fights.

Similarly, student sexual harassment through fondling and other unwanted tactile contacts is another problem that has intensified in recent years. Many folks used to laugh it off as inept attempts at romancing, but no more.

Most schools have now developed programs or implemented published programs that purport to train students in assertiveness, reduce the stereotyping and harassment of targeted individuals and small groups of students, teach anger management, and the like. How sad that it's become necessary to legalize and institutionalize such a fundamental human relationship as touch, but that's the way it is. Furthermore, we don't want good-touch/bad-touch rhetoric to frighten young children away from positive physical contacts with adults, and we don't want the informal rough-and-tumble of school life that's generally positive to escalate into the bullying and fighting that's almost always negative, but that's the way it is. It's thus very important that we truly involve students in the discussion of such problems and in the collaborative proposal and implementation of solutions. They're part of the problem; they ought to be part of the solution.

CHANGE AS PSYCHOLOGICAL MOVEMENT

Our large frontal lobes allow us to experience movement as a psychological as well as a physical phenomenon. People physically move from one community to another, but they also then change jobs and may psychologically shift to a different career level. Children are also involved in such career-related family moves, and they're often unhappy about it. Moves can be especially difficult for children whose parents' vocation requires multiple moves (such as those in the military, large corporations, the clergy, and sports). Furthermore, current vocational patterns suggest that most people will change jobs (and even vocations) several times during their career, so the problem will probably continue. If it's a positive career-related move to another community, the parental delight over the move may further exacerbate their children's unhappiness (as occurred once within our family during a career-related move that delighted my wife and me but not our children).

Our brain responds most strongly to high-contrast information, and it can activate stress responses when such information seems threatening. Holmes and Rahe (1967) found that the most stressful (high-contrast) life changes involve the loss of family and friends and the prospect of having to make new friends, and so children who move from their community and school experience a lot of psychologically threatening goodbye-and-hello activity. Students who depart and arrive during the school year are therefore generally experiencing a period of high stress (and perhaps the variety of physical ailments that often accompany high stress). The situation is similar with students who will move or have moved during the summer. Chapter 6 introduced the concept of a responsive curriculum, and the discussion that follows suggests that the physical and psychological shifts that students experience are certainly an important part of this curriculum and ought to be recognized in the classroom if it's appropriate.

It's important to help young people make the transition as smoothly as possible. In our family's case, a generous phone policy and trips back to see friends helped the transition, but e-mail and the Internet now provide marvelous, inexpensive keep-in-touch possibilities that didn't exist a few years ago (and school-to-school e-mail connections during a transition work well for students without a computer at home).

It's very difficult to provide extended support to transient students in schools with an unusually high turnover rate during the school year, but a class that goes through the process only a few times a year can be quite helpful to their departing classmates. Encourage students who are moving to check out their new community on the Internet and in the public library and to request material on the community from the chamber of commerce. Check to see if any staff or students in your school have lived in the community to which your student is moving, and bring the two together. If your student's family has already secured housing and knows which school your student will attend, contact his or her future class via e-mail and begin the student's *hello* process prior to arrival. Encourage your student to prepare a class report on the community since such a project typically develops a more positive attitude about the move.

Continue class contact via e-mail after the move. The contacts will taper off as your former student develops new friends, but close friends will probably stay in contact longer via e-mail if you encourage it. Send a copy of the room diary (see Suggested Activities, Chapter 6) to students who moved during the school year or (if you don't develop a room diary) develop a collaborative end-of-the-year report to send to all students who moved during the year.

It's equally important to create procedures for welcoming new students into your classroom. The entire class is new at the beginning of the school year, but some students already know each other because they were classmates last year and/or are neighborhood friends. Others will have moved into the community during the summer or are transferring from another community school. Schedule many group activities during the first weeks, mixing the already acquainted with the truly new in a variety of groupings. Ask the new students to tell the class about their previous community and friends. Develop activities that help students to identify their interests and abilities, and then create class groups that reflect such commonalities.

Divide your class into host committees of four students. Each committee should serve for a month or so to welcome and assist any students who arrive during their tenure. These *formal first friends* may not become the permanent friends of the new students, but developing some kind of system to help students get acquainted certainly smoothes the process.

Death, divorce, and a major drop in family income are examples of other psychological moves that can greatly grieve students. They often signal the end of the life a person had been living. Students may or may not want tell you about their problems, but teachers commonly become aware of the significant life changes their students are experiencing.

Part of the problem that children confront is that their primary caregivers are often also traumatized by the event and so may not be able to effectively help them through the grief process. Children, feeling a mixed bag of experiences and emotions (such as loss, betrayal, anger, and sadness), may not know how to respond and so withdraw. Adults may interpret this as a lack of feeling or that the child is doing fine, but the reality is that the child is typically devastated and confused. It's also important to realize that a loss that may seem trivial to an adult (such as the death of a pet or the loss of a favorite toy) may be very important to your student.

Let your grieving student know by words and action that you are aware of and genuinely concerned about the situation. Carefully observe your student's behavior, and always make time to listen when your student wants to talk. Be sensitive to different students and situations—a family death typically doesn't embarrass a child, but a divorce or the parental loss of a job might. Bibliotherapy can often help grieving students since such children's books allow readers to privately explore their personal grief through the story's narrative (Rousell, 1992). Ask librarians for suggestions of good storybooks that focus on the loss your student is experiencing. Finally, the effort expended to create a caring classroom really pays off when students grieve. They discover that people they live with 6 hours a day are developing into a support group for each other, and the grieving student can see others providing the support that he or she would provide to classmates if the conditions were reversed.

This chapter began with the joyful centrality of movement in our lives, and it concludes with the sad ending of movement that occurs in such events as hitting and dying. Movement is an intriguing enigma. Sometimes so many people want to simultaneously move quickly along a street that gridlock seriously slows the process, and anger seethes. Conversely, people may later line the sidewalks of the same street in a celebratory mood to observe a parade that also moves very slowly. We'll spend several minutes driving through a mall parking lot to find a space near an entrance when we could have immediately parked slightly further away and walked to the entrance and back in much less time. People who are impressed by TV commercials of sports utility vehicles bouncing over rugged terrain buy one and never drive it off paved roads. People save money for a vacation to get away from it all, travel 1,000 miles to another city, and stay in a franchise motel, eat in franchise restaurants, visit franchise-dominated malls, and see films—all of which are available in their home community. Why did they leave home? When we're here, we often want to be there. When we're young, we want to look grown up, and when we're old, we want things to look young. We truly are crazy about movement!

SUGGESTED ACTIVITIES

The activities below explore some of the slow-to-fast movement patterns that occur across a school year and so can spark discussions about the concept of movement that could lead to collaborative management adaptations. Since movement combines space and time, some of these activities are also appropriate for exploring space and time.

Weight and Height

Growth is so gradual that most of us are unaware of it. If you measure and/or weigh the entire class once a week and graph the total, the graph will provide the class with an amazing and amusing view of their total growth over the year. (A fifth-grade class of 25 students may grow a combined total of 6-plus feet and add 200 pounds over the course of the school year, almost the equivalent of a couple additional students.) Primary grades can graph their total weekly loss of teeth, and other classes may come up with other interesting movement-related things in their lives that can be graphed in their weekly totality. These graphs aren't a good activity with a class that contains students who might be sensitive about the factors being measured and graphed.

An Event Clock

Post a strip of paper about 1 foot wide and 7 feet long on a wall. Divide the length from top down into 15-minute intervals from the beginning to the end of the school day (write 8:00, 8:15, 8:30, etc. down the left side). Ask your students to notice events that occur about the same time every day (a passing mail truck, a scheduled commercial plane flying overhead, the first whiff of the cafeteria smells, a class going to the gym). Check each candidate event for several days to ensure its regularity, and then insert the event into the closest 15-minute slot on the event clock. The clock will usually fill up with predictable events by the end of the school year, but it may become a real challenge in May to locate predictable events for the few unfilled slots. The activity gives you two classroom clocks: a chronological clock and an amusing event clock that charts how things move across the day ("The mailman has arrived, so it's just about time for PE").

Lumber Use

Give each of your students a pencil the first day of school. The writing part of a pencil (up to the metal eraser cap) is generally 6.75 inches, so it's relatively easy to measure how much pencil space the class will use during a week.

Place a pad by the wastebasket, and ask students to make a tally for every sheet of paper they throw in the wastebasket. Graph the amount of paper that moves into and out of your classroom.

Move It

It's fun to develop timed competitions in which teams of students try to move something through an obstacle course without actually touching it. For example, give each of three team members a drinking straw and the challenge to use the straws to move a ping pong ball over a prescribed course. They can blow on the ball, collaborate on trying to pick it up and carry it with their three straws, or devise any other approach that doesn't involve team members physically touching it. Your class will devise all sorts of other imaginative challenges that limit the resources they can use to move something, such as using a yard of string to move a soccer ball up a flight of stairs.

Help your students discover that these activities do naturally what video games do electronically—move something (such as the game characters) from here to there in the face of obstacles. But then, don't golf, tennis, baseball, and hockey also use implements to move objects from here to there?

Distant Friends

Insert pins into a map of the country to represent every community where your students have relatives, are in contact with through e-mail friends, or have visited.

CHAPTER EIGHT

Collaboratively Managing Biological and Cultural Range

We could theoretically live decades beyond our current human life span and confront any possible challenge, but that capability would come at an enormous biological cost. We would need back-up and regenerative systems for everything, a fail-safe immune system and protective mechanisms for larger external and internal dangers, and a much larger bodybrain than we currently have to continuously support all this extra capability.

We could similarly design our machines to last far longer and function more efficiently than they typically do, but it's doubtful that we could then afford them. For example, consider the current high average per mile cost of purchasing and maintaining the very best engineered automobiles. The more complex the task of a technology, the greater the maintenance costs and potential for an eventual costly breakdown. On the other hand, we can use spoons, bottle openers, and other simple but important limited-use technologies for many decades without any need for repair.

We humans have many complex body parts and systems, but we can still live to about 100 years, eat a wide variety of plants and animals, live in crowded communities, and survive in a thermal range of more than 100 degrees. Our maintenance costs for being able to live a long life in a worldwide ecological range are very high, though, compared to early humans who lived less than half our average life span in a far simpler environment. Consider how much of our energy (translated into income) we use to pay for such needs as food, clothing, shelter, travel, and medical costs. We've further used our considerable cognitive abilities to develop technologies that compensate for our biological limitations. For example, we've developed travel, shelter, medical, and food preparation technologies to augment our bodybrain's capabilities and to extend our ecological range and life span.

The trade-off in both biology and technology is to balance cost and benefit—to provide for whatever is necessary to carry out the desired function but to not go very far beyond that. Recent lawsuits against car manufacturers have alleged that the companies deliberately used cheaper parts than what was available and that the malfunction of the cheap parts caused the accidents that killed the driver and/or passengers. That decision was allegedly made because the manufacturer determined that it would cost less to settle the lawsuits from a potentially small number of accidents than to purchase the more expensive part for the many cars it intended to manufacture. We're appalled at such reasoning, but then we do try to spend as little money as possible when purchasing a car.

Schools must constantly make similarly difficult cost/benefit decisions. Our patrons expect us to accomplish a lot (a wide benefit range) but to do it as cheaply and efficiently as possible (a narrow cost range). It's unfair but common for patrons to then complain when educators are forced to make choices that eliminate staff and programs that would benefit their children. If we want the cost/benefit ratio to favor economy, we must realize that a cheap car is a cheap car, and a cheap education is a cheap education. It shouldn't be difficult to understand that a reduced investment in something also typically reduces its range of possibilities and overall effectiveness.

But could schools accomplish everything one could hope for if we had unlimited resources and staff? Probably not. Expending money to expand the effective range of something doesn't necessarily ensure perfection. Like cars, we humans have some critically important systems (such as circulation and respiration) that seem to give out eventually while other systems (such as skin and skeleton) typically continue to function well at our death. The body and engine of most cars and humans are excellent, but they're not perfect. We can spend a lot of money to maintain the health of our heart and/or lungs and practically no money on our skin and bones and still die of heart or lung failure. Schools can similarly expend a lot of energy on students who are well below the normal range in ability and/or behavior, but that doesn't ensure success in moving them into the normal range, if that's the goal. But it also doesn't mean that we should simply give up on them.

The biological cost/benefit ratio suggests that the general biological imperative for plants and animals is to stay alive long enough and to do whatever it takes to get into the gene pool. We bear dependent children, so we have a bodybrain that is generally up to the task of staying alive through our reproductive cycle and then long enough beyond it to complete the extended rearing of any children we have (and as a social species, we also participate in rearing the children of others). A great serendipity of the recent biologically expensive advances in medicine, diet, shelter, and so on is that many of us now live long enough to also enjoy our grandchildren and great grandchildren (which my grandparents couldn't do), but it does take us beyond our normal biological expectations.

Our inevitable death may finally result from the limited number of times body cells can divide—perhaps up to 100 times (mature neurons don't divide, and cancer involves unchecked cell division). Cells in the aged that have reached their limit in division can continue to carry out their functions but won't divide, and so they become more susceptible to medical problems that can lead to death (K. Wright, 2002).

What's biologically possible and what's culturally appropriate are the two principal issues we humans face as we compete to stay alive and get into the gene pool (culturally appropriate behavior tending to enhance mating attractiveness). The concepts of biological possibility and cultural appropriateness presuppose that our capabilities and behavior operate within somewhat definable functional and acceptable personal and social ranges.

This chapter will thus focus on the final behavioral element in the biological and cultural underpinnings of collaborative classroom management. Biological systems function through the expenditure of *energy* within our *space/time* world, which generally causes physical and psychological *movement* within biological and cultural *ranges*.

This examination of range finally gets us into personal and social identity and into perhaps the three most important of Gardner's

(1998) nine categories of intelligence: intrapersonal, interpersonal, and existential intelligence—Who am I? Who are these people around me? What does it mean to exist?

Since issues surrounding classroom management focus principally on determining the reasonable range of possible and appropriate movement (or behavior) in a classroom, it's important for educators and students to understand (and explore) the concept of biological and cultural range as they relate to identity. The two examples that follow should spark classroom and collegial exploratory thought and discussion.

1. An individual light fixture typically functions within a very narrow illumination range. It's either on or off. It has no almost-on state, and most fixtures have no dimming capabilities. We decide how much illumination we want the fixture to produce and then use a bulb with that intensity. Similarly, an individual neuron activates only if the incoming molecular information reaches the cell's current firing threshold, and it typically remains inactive otherwise. It's a narrow-range, all-or-nothing operating system that, like a light bulb, is tuned to the needs of its specific task.

Conversely, our brain's complex of 100-plus billion neurons allows it to function more like a room with many on/off light fixtures of various intensities that together can create a wide range of light intensities and shadows. I recently sat transfixed in a theater as the complex lighting system (with its on/off, dimming, placement, and color capabilities) intensified and enhanced the positive-to-negative range of the elements in a play that would have been a considerably different experience had the stage lighting been severely limited and unchanging. The story would have been told, but much of the theatrical magic would have been absent. On the other hand, spectacular lighting that overwhelms the play can be counterproductive. Just right (whatever that is) is best. Tune the system to the task.

Our brain's total level of activation similarly depends on which and how many neurons are actively responding to the current challenges. An individual neuron is thus a very limited on/off system, but a total brain has a very wide and continually shifting range of cognitive states (as brain scans graphically demonstrate). Similarly, an entire collaborative classroom full of individually limited brains sparks thoughts of the wide range of constantly changing light intensities that highlight the stage area where a play is being performed.

The constantly shifting behavioral intensities that so characterize classroom management problems may thus be the theatrical magic of a school day, highlighting individual activity within the range of constantly changing positive-to-negative curricular and behavioral elements. What are the possible and appropriate ranges of intensity? That's the problem a theatrical director and classroom teacher constantly confront, and fortunately, there's no one way to light a play or to manage a classroom. How dull life would be if things were that simple and absolute.

2. Range issues are everywhere. Let's use something as mundane as this page to explore another element of the concept of range. The words on this page could have been printed so they would reach to all four edges, but it's not possible to print them beyond the edges. The page dimensions thus define the possible range. Although it's possible to print to the edge, we typically leave a margin between text and edge since it aids in binding the pages if it's a multiple-page document, and margins allow for margin notes. Whatever the original reason for margins, they're familiar, and so we've become comfortable with them and expect them.

The issue of the size of the margin gets to the heart of appropriateness. One-inch margins on all sides are probably the default margin (and a requirement for certain manuscripts). But we often reduce the margins to fit all the text of a letter that's slightly longer than a page onto a single page, or we may expand the margins to center a short letter on a page. We may also extend the margin size of a small section of text to set it off from the rest. So margin decisions may be based on an artificial requirement or on what's aesthetically pleasing to whomever gets to determine the margin size.

We further commonly change the margins for headings and to signal the beginning and ending of a paragraph. The first (indented) line of the paragraph has a wider left margin, and the end of the paragraph often stops short of the normal right margin. That's the common practice, but it's also appropriate to double space (without indenting) to separate paragraphs.

But suppose someone decides to simply print an extended manuscript as a single long paragraph, sentence following sentence following sentence—and simply uses an icon (such as *) to identify the first sentence of each new paragraph. The text wouldn't have changed at all, and the signal for a new paragraph is certainly clear.

It's readable, but most of us wouldn't like it. It's a possible but unfamiliar procedure, and so we'd probably consider it inappropriate, simply because it's unfamiliar.

It may be that the cost/benefit ratio concept is so deeply ingrained in us that we automatically and often unconsciously compute it in most challenges we face, even such as how easy it is to read the text on a page compared to the value of the material. Our cost/benefit computations typically lead us to a comfortable acceptable range, even though we realize that our acceptable range is quite subjective and perhaps narrower or wider than the acceptable range of others.

In a complex society, some folks want to extend a given normal behavioral range; others don't. Think of a freeway with posted speed limits of 45 to 65 mph. Most people don't consider it serious if someone travels slightly beyond the range at 44 or 66, but traveling at 30 or 80 may attract honking and gesturing (as ironically will driving in the passing lane at exactly the posted speed). Folks who travel the freeway at 75 rather than 65 save only 10 to 15 minutes during a 100-mile trip. It's perhaps hardly worth the risk and effort, but it's understandable if the cost/benefit goal isn't to save a few minutes but rather to simply enjoy the stimulation of driving fast. My favorite bumper sticker in this category is "I may be slow, but I'm ahead of you."

Normal. Familiar. Comfortable. We consider these very important interrelated factors when we make decisions about the range of the acceptable. They all assume a somewhat flexible range of what's acceptable, and so they allow us to quickly (and often unconsciously) choose among alternatives. Things generally don't have to be exact, just close—within our comfort range. If one color for a purchase isn't available, we'll take another (if color isn't the critical factor). But it's also important to realize that normal, familiar, and comfortable are mental states that can lead to exclusions based on a range influenced by racist, sexist, and/or elitist values.

Advertising often exploits our preference for familiar comfortable normality. In the advertising world, we confront familiar problems through images that we can easily relate to. Everything is normal in the scenario except the product, which is abnormally cheaper (cost) and/or better (benefit) than its competition—a little abnormal seasoning in a big pot of comfortable familiar normality. Better yet, let's connect a comfortable children's film to burgers-and-fries ads, a familiar TV football analyst to our hardware chain, or a normal activity such as driving a car to our roaring-up-the-mountain sports utility vehicle, and our ad will spice up comfort, familiarity, and normality with a little celebrity and excitement. Still better, tie a product icon to the entire scenario, and then all we have to do is display the swoosh or the golden arches, and everyone will settle comfortably into familiar normality.

Figure 8.1 illustrates the concept of range. It identifies a normal range area and high/low abnormal levels separated by leaky horizontal lines (semipermeable membranes, no less) that illustrate the frequent difficulty of clearly establishing the point at which normality becomes abnormality. Abnormal performance can become a pathology if it moves far enough beyond the normal range, and anything at that level is typically more expensive to make (a critical machine part that could kill someone if it malfunctions) or to maintain (a penitentiary inmate). Technological assistance (such as medication or a wheelchair) is often used to improve the behavior of a low-performing abnormality and to dampen above-normal performance that's negative (such as medication for schizophrenia). Above-normal behavior that is considered positive (virtuoso behavior) is also often technologically augmented (such as with food supplements and exercise equipment for athletes) in an attempt to move the behavior even further beyond normality.

Work with your students to identify classroom management issues that exist within a range of possible behaviors, such as what clothing students may wear in school or the level of participation in class discussions. Identify behavioral examples that would be at the two ends of the acceptable range, and then insert other examples along a continuum within and beyond the range.

To demonstrate range with a simple (quartile) activity, ask all of your students to sequentially throw a ball as far as they can along the same trajectory. Mark the spot where each ball lands (without identifying students with the markers). Divide the number of throws by 4. Count off and mark the fourth of the throws that are the longest and shortest. The middle half of the throws could be considered the normal range, and the shortest and longest fourths could be considered beyond the normal range. The throw that falls at the mid-value of all throws is called the *median*.

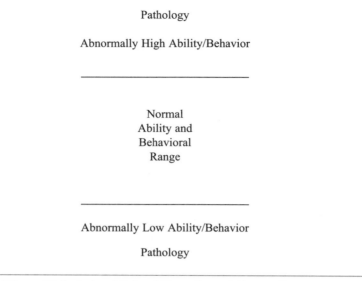

Pathology

Abnormally High Ability/Behavior

Normal
Ability and
Behavioral
Range

Abnormally Low Ability/Behavior

Pathology

Figure 8.1   Biological and Cultural Normality and Abnormality

BIOLOGICALLY POSSIBLE RANGES

As suggested earlier, it's not biologically sound for any human ability or behavior to function within an almost limitless range. The cost/benefit ratio just doesn't compute. The Olympic Games represent our glorious worldwide attempt to extend the range of human movement. So some folks spend much of their youth trying to lengthen the human jumping range by one more inch, but most of us who want to go higher than we currently are simply use a ladder. It's an issue of personal identity.

As indicated in the activity above, we can assemble a normally distributed collection of students along almost any ability and performance range. For whatever reason, about two-thirds will typically fall within the defined normal range in bell-shaped curve computations, and the others will spread out into the high and low abnormal ranges. It's possible that the normal range of many abilities eventually emerged (in some ill-understood way) out of a biologically favorable cost/benefit ratio related to the general imperative to stay alive and get into the gene pool, and that's why so many folks end up within the normal range. Being in the normal range in that ability would simplify our life and reduce the energy we need to carry out a task that we're now biologically tuned into. By extension, having a whole classroom full of normally behaving students certainly reduces the energy a teacher must expend in working with them.

We've tended to put more of our energy into designing educational programs for normal students than for the abnormally high and low. Again, the cost/benefit ratio often favors such a focus for teachers. The much larger number of students in the normal range in a given ability has provided our profession with many years of useful normative information on student capability and instructional preference. Much of this is folklore knowledge, but it drives much of what we do. If most of our students are more or less capable of carrying out our planned (normal range) instructional task, it's almost as if we only have to teach one multihead student, and so a one-size-fits-all instructional approach provides us a great cost/benefit ratio. But what if we misjudge the group's ability? Not to worry. Students have this marvelous feedback system called misbehavior to let us know if we've overshot or undershot their ability and interest range. Tweak the lesson plan and continue.

Unfortunately, designing curriculum and instruction principally for students in the normal range almost ensures by definition that much of it will be too difficult for the abnormally low and not challenging enough for the abnormally high. Grades and disciplinary measures are, alas, one way of transferring the blame for low performance to the student. A major task in the years ahead will be to develop better diagnostic tools of student ability and individualized computer programs in curricular areas in which we currently teach an individually mastered veridical skill (such as spelling or the multiplication tables) in a whole-class setting. There's nothing social about spelling or the multiplication tables. Whole-class instruction could then focus on true socially and preference-oriented curricular areas and issues such as the arts and humanities, in which a precise performance standard is of less concern than the exploration of different ways to confront a concept. Science and social studies projects are another area in which a broad range of student ability can function effectively in a group setting. And we have yet to develop a truly effective social behavior curriculum. Finally, this book has argued throughout that teachers can reduce many of their problems by simply collaborating with their students in the design and execution of as many curricular, instructional, and management tasks as possible. Doing this doesn't eliminate problems; it just trades one set of problems for another, but problems that emerge out of classroom collaboration are more stimulating.

U.S. schools have invested far more money per student in trying to increase the performance of the abnormally low than the abnormally high. It may be a matter of (perhaps unconsciously) wanting to move the abnormally low into normal levels and of being somewhat disinterested in moving the abnormally high even further from normality.

Singapore, on the other hand, invests heavily in programs for talented and gifted students, in the belief that they're investing in the economic and political future of their country by providing their best students with the best educational opportunities. The U.S. decision may partially reflect the belief that the mark of a society is in how it treats those who are most in need of help. Note that two economically successful countries computed the educational cost/benefit ratio differently. The ideal policy would obviously be to create excellent programs across the entire normal and abnormal range (but it's difficult to negotiate cost/benefit ratios in a highly politicized institution).

Why are some students in the abnormal range? For a long time, people thought motivation and perseverance were the key elements—the abnormally high and low were the conscious cause of their own condition. Recent developments suggest that it's more complex than that. Performance can be affected by such developmental factors as the robustness of the pathways that connect related brain areas and the production and distribution of neurotransmitters. For our purposes at this point, let's focus on neurochemical normality and abnormality.

Some 60 neurotransmitter systems play key roles in regulating cognitive activity, and abnormally high or low basal levels of a neurotransmitter can affect ability and performance in the areas the neurotransmitter helps to regulate.

Dopamine is an important neurotransmitter that's involved in the regulation of various behaviors. Low dopamine levels have been associated with Parkinson's disease and attention deficit disorders. Conversely, high dopamine levels have been associated with such maladies as schizophrenia, Tourette's syndrome, and obsessive-compulsive disorder. Medical interventions seek to move abnormal levels into the normal range—for example, L-dopa and other medications are prescribed to boost dopamine levels for patients with Parkinson's disease, and neuroleptics are used to reduce dopamine levels in patients with schizophrenia.

Chapter 4 discussed serotonin, which plays an important role in regulating movement. Low serotonin levels lead to uncoordinated awkward movements that tend to lower self-esteem (given the social importance of our motor system), and high serotonin levels lead to smoothly coordinated movements that tend to enhance one's self-esteem. Furthermore, low serotonin levels have been associated with such maladies as depression and bulimia, and high serotonin levels have been associated with anorexia. The fluoxetine antidepressants (such as Prozac) boost serotonin effectiveness, but as indicated earlier, we've also long self-medicated with alcohol, carbohydrates, and herbal remedies (such as St. John's wort) to boost moderately low serotonin levels.

Given that the other five dozen neurotransmitters also play important roles in determining a wide variety of abilities and behaviors, it's becoming more obvious that if basal neurotransmitter levels are at least partially innate, not everyone has a biologically equal opportunity to function easily within the normal optimum neurochemical range, and this should certainly affect classroom management expectations and practices. The biological energy the chemically abnormal students must expend to function within a school's preferred normal behavioral range will reduce the energy they have available for other functions, such as what's needed for curricular tasks.

When chemical systems are imbalanced, the point of a medical intervention is to get the systems back in chemical balance and not to blame or punish the patient. Similarly, when classroom behavior is inappropriate, the principal point of the management intervention should be to restore behavioral balance in student and class. Management procedures that do this shouldn't focus on punishment but rather on helping the student(s) to understand the logical consequences of the behavior and repair what went wrong. It comes down to this: if something is broken, fix it rather than complain about it.

Abnormality in an area isn't necessarily totally negative. Chapter 5 suggested that an abnormally low ability in one area may lead to a compensating strength in a related area, a biologically sensible solution for an organism that needs to combine all its resources as best it can to function effectively. For example, some people whose brains can't rapidly process high-contrast visual information (such as reading black words on a white page) have abnormal spatial abilities that manifest themselves in superior performance in athletics and the visual arts. We're fascinated by such virtuoso abnormalities and often pay them well to entertain us, despite their inadequacies in other performance areas.

The increased interest in such developments as cooperative learning, multiple intelligences, and learning styles attests to our profession's growing awareness that biological diversity itself can be a valuable property in a social group. If the different overlapping ability ranges in a class are respected for what they can provide, the aggregate of the individual ranges will expand the corporate range at no increased biological cost.

The ability level of most bodybrain systems is generally in the abnormally low range at birth. Some systems, such as circulation and respiration, must be functionally normal at birth, and some survival abilities, such as to suckle, come on line almost immediately after birth with no prior instruction or experience (although fetal thumb sucking does occur).

We can move our hands and legs at birth, but we can't grasp or walk. Mobility is an important human capability, so as Chapter 7 suggested, our motor system develops quickly from the low abnormal level into the normal range. Most children walk by the age of 1. The maturation of most aspects of the motor system across the normal ability range is an important first-decade task.

One of our more intriguing cognitive abilities is to abstract one property out of an object regardless of what the object is. For example, even a small child can recognize the redness of a red rose or crayon and the roundness of a ball or a plate.

Similarly, we can easily determine the quantity of a collection of objects (such as three boxes) regardless of differences in size, shape, use, and so forth. Recent discoveries suggest that this ability to enumerate is processed in a left (and probably also right) hemisphere brain area called the inferior parietal cortex (or angular gyrus) at the juncture of the occipital, temporal, and parietal lobes (Butterworth, 1999). We can determine the quantity of up to four objects with a quick glance (called subitizing), but we must count out larger quantities (and we generally count by ones, twos, or threes). Check it out with various collections of objects in the room to see which ones you can quantify with a quick noncounting glance.

Four-month-old infants readily differentiate among such small quantities. This seemingly innate ability represents the lower edge of our normal ability range in processing quantity. The neuronal networks that process quantities up to four thus become our mathematical womb. Neuronal systems near our brain's numerical module are recruited through childhood and beyond to expand the range of our ability to quantify from simple counting (aided by our fingers, which are also represented in the parietal lobes) to arithmetic computation to more complex mathematical problems.

Neurons in this cortical area were more densely packed than normal in Albert Einstein's brain. Butterworth (1999) reported several cases of people who suffered highly specific losses in numerical ability because of a stroke in this region that only destroyed certain specialized neurons. One woman lost her ability to subitize and could not count beyond four. Mathematics is a very complex human capability, but it all emerges from a simple innate brain module and its cognitive properties.

It's thus not surprising that we're generally most comfortable and effective when manipulating the lower numbers that were with us at birth. Primary teachers have long realized that it's easier for children to learn such multiplication facts as 2×3 than 9×7, despite the fact that the two memory tasks are similar. We further tend to reduce large complex quantities to small simpler sets, especially to sets of three (Father, Son, Holy Ghost; id, ego, superego; legislative, executive, judicial). When asked why people tend to group complex phenomena into three categories, intelligence theorist Robert Sternberg (of triarchic brain theory fame) wryly responded, "Well, there are three reasons. . . ."

To revisit and expand on our developmental trajectory briefly introduced in Chapter 5, we have a modular brain, and all cognitive abilities begin with a basic, survival-level version of the mature module that processes the ability. The environment stimulates this protosystem, and it tends to develop quickly initially with limited instruction and effort from an abnormally low level into the low-normal range. For example, we're absolutely fascinated by the rapid development of speech during the preschool years, from random babbling to articulate speech (with no explicit instruction in such language complexities as prepositional phrases and plurals). Mastery is enhanced by a rich verbal environment in which the names of things are often visually associated with the objects and actions. A parent says, "Drink your milk out of this cup" while giving the child the cup.

Certain brain systems of some children are initially much less competent than normal. A child's auditory system can normally recognize sounds that are only 10 milliseconds (ms) apart. Since stop consonants (such as *b, p,* and *k*) require 40 ms and vowels 100 ms, a normal auditory system can easily separate and process the various phonemes in a word, and so such children's phonemic systems mature quickly in the welter of words they constantly hear. Conversely, children who are language learning delayed (LLD) have an auditory system that can only recognize sounds that are maybe 250 ms apart (a quarter of a second), so words are just jumbled sounds to them. Speech development becomes seriously delayed. Chapter 2 mentioned the Fast ForWord program (Scientific Learning Corporation, 1997) as a successful intervention that uses video game technology to speed up auditory processing in such children, to move them into the normal range needed to process speech. It's probable that many other computerized skill development technologies will emerge in the foreseeable future, tuned to the very specific developmental needs of the entire range of normal and abnormal students.

More complex aspects of a cognitive ability don't come as easily and generally require explicit instruction and extended practice to make the neural connections that mature the system. While speech seems to emerge naturally, reading must be explicitly taught because it requires visual and auditory connections that are far more abstract. Translating "drink your milk out of this cup" into a collection of vertical, horizontal, diagonal, and curved lines on a sheet of paper with no cup in sight doesn't enhance immediate mastery.

The situation is similar with other abilities. Walking is almost automatic, but tap dancing must be taught and is mastered with difficulty. The startle reflex is innate, but children have to be taught how to cross busy streets and avoid sharp things. Very young children use a melody to easily memorize our alphabetic sequence of 26 unrelated letters, but they have to be taught how to play a violin.

Cognitive ranges have an upper normal limit, and we tend to use augmenting technologies when faced with mastering a task that requires effort beyond a comfortable biological cost/benefit ratio. So children who mentally mastered the multiplication tables up to 12 use a paper-and-pencil equation or a calculator to multiply larger numbers. Children who can run quite fast for short distances use skates and bicycles to travel faster and farther. Children who easily learned the difficult alphabet sequence prefer to use a phone book instead of memorizing all their friends' phone numbers.

As suggested earlier, virtuosos and savants expend considerable energy to extend performance in an area well beyond the normal human range. A virtuoso is superior in one ability and at least within the normal range in most others. A savant is superior in one ability and is generally below normal in most other abilities. Many savants are autistic. Such superior performance often comes at the expense of other abilities, as the cost/benefit ratio suggests. Since much of our cognitive energy is directed toward processing social skills, the networks that process social skills (interpersonal intelligence) would be the most likely to suffer in the neuronal competitions, when some other specific ability is developed far beyond the normal range. Autism exhibits a serious interpersonal deficit, and virtuosos often (but certainly not always) exhibit interpersonal deficiencies—lauded by the masses but perhaps not by their family and associates.

CULTURALLY APPROPRIATE RANGES

Being biologically able to do something differs from the issue of whether we should do it. The discussion immediately above raises serious questions about the intense training required of children who seek (or whose parents seek) world-class status in some endeavor in which they have considerable ability. I'm amazed by what children can do in the Olympics, for example, but I'm also concerned about the loss in social development that results from intense individualized training and about the long-range effects of such training on an immature body pushed well beyond its normal range.

Ability is an individual biological phenomenon, but appropriateness typically involves behavior with strong social and cultural overtones. Like ability, the appropriateness of various behaviors extends along the normal and abnormal range illustrated in Figure 8.1.

Children typically grow up in an intensely social environment in which they constantly receive (often conflicting) messages about appropriate behavior from parents and peers. A social species depends on a somewhat equitable sharing of effort and resources, and so our culture strongly promotes a tit-for-tat mentality in children as a central element of social development. Any parent will attest that it's not an easy sell—the child grumbles at the request to do a minor chore, only hours after the parent made some major desired purchase for the child. One problem with getting young children to freely share is that their lives involve a very unequal dependent relationship. Others give and they take, and they get used to that arrangement. It's thus not surprising that children are self-centered.

A collaborative approach to classroom management moves students into an arena beyond the informality of their family and involves them in complex social problems that will enhance their understanding of cost/benefit ratios and help them to develop a tit-for-tat orientation. It's important for our culture that children mature into altruistic adults who are able and willing to contribute their share and beyond for the common good. The school is simply an excellent laboratory for developing this.

We certainly all know adults who haven't matured beyond their childhood self-centeredness. They often insist, for example, that governmental services be increased and taxes decreased, despite the irrationality of their position. When challenged, they tend to ridicule governmental inefficiency to bolster a weak argument that it's easy to accomplish more with less. (How many bureaucrats does it take to screw in a lightbulb? Two: one to reassure the citizens that the problem is being solved and another to screw the bulb into a water faucet.) It's important for us to realize that all such critics went through our school system and that the next potential set is currently sitting in classroom desks. How much better it is to help them to understand the complexity of social processes now than to be very frustrated later by their simplistic complaints and solutions.

We use verbal and nonverbal means to communicate our assessment of the appropriateness of other people's behavior. As the person's behavior moves toward the negative end of our range, we use frowns and reprimands, and when the behavior moves across the line into the abnormally inappropriate range, we shift to stronger expressions of anger and disgust. Conversely, as a person's behavior becomes better than normal, we use smiles and encouragement, and when it becomes abnormally positive, we break out in laughter and effuse praise. And finally, if our behavior is more or less appropriate for years on end, we generally get a framed certificate upon retirement (in my case, with my name misspelled).

It's in the self-interest of children to become proficient at reading the language and body language of their significant adults to determine the current range of appropriate behavior and their position in it. Children who live in a family with a clearly defined constant normal range learn to tune their behavior to expectations they understand. Children who live with inconsistent parents often have no clear, consistent guide to what's appropriate. Both kinds of children will constantly explore the edges of appropriateness (just as adults go slightly over the speed limit and show up a bit late for work and do other things to discover how far they can go over the line without reprimand). The children in the secure environment learn from their forays to the edge of the normal range, but the other children don't because the range constantly shifts in their home.

Getting caught going over the line isn't necessarily negative in a child's life if it helps to clarify the point at which appropriate behavior becomes inappropriate. Calmly discussing the logical consequences of the behavior is the best way to help children to understand why their behavior is inappropriate and to repair the damage they caused.

Children bring to school what they've learned at home, and as students they similarly become adept at knowing their teacher's view of where the normal limits of appropriate behavior are. Those who are slow at picking up such signals generally experience a lot of grief with their teachers.

It's important that students learn that the dividing line between what's appropriate and inappropriate is subjective, but it can still require compliance. Traffic laws provide many good illustrations. For example, the law can't argue that it's logically better to drive on either the right or the left side of the street, but it can logically insist that everyone going the same direction must drive on the same side. If we've stopped at a stoplight, and absolutely no traffic is coming from any direction, should we wait for the green signal? Is it all right for a pedestrian at a *wait* signal to *walk* if no cars are in sight? Is it inappropriate for a driver going straight to pull up to a stoplight in the right lane and so prevent drivers behind him from making a right turn during the red light? We confront situations like these all the time.

Humor and the arts are perhaps so culturally pervasive because they both help us to constantly explore the dividing line between appropriate and inappropriate behavior in pretend rather than in real-life situations (such as with the traffic signal problems above).

We especially need to constantly explore the subtle shifts and discrepancies that move behaviors beyond the dividing line.

Our right frontal lobe contains modules that apparently process discrepancies (especially in linguistic information) and then pass such information on to our emotional thermostat, and this leads to automatic responses (such as laughter and anger) that signal the increased vigor of our assessment of the appropriateness of the situation. Since the frontal lobes of young children aren't mature, they generally respond best to (and laugh at) broad discrepancies, such as in slapstick humor, rather than at subtle puns and other forms of word play that adults with mature frontal lobes enjoy. Young children can thus recognize very inappropriate behavior, but they often find it difficult to make fine discriminations and appropriate judgments of their own behavior.

Students generally include "a sense of humor" when asked to identify preferred teacher characteristics. This suggests that students (perhaps unconsciously) appreciate teachers who can recognize student behavior that's getting close to or is right over the line and respond (at least initially) with a communicative smile or wink rather than a premature expression of anger. Insert this understanding of humor into your explorations of classroom management. Seeing the inappropriateness to absurdity of a situation with an expression that signals humor can defuse many a tense classroom confrontation of what or who is right.

The comedian Stephen Wright is known for his absurd but subtle jokes, many of which revolve around a play on a single word. "I got interested in astronomy, and so I installed a skylight. The people in the apartment above me are furious." "If the cops arrest a mime, do they have to tell him he has the right to remain silent?" The subtle turn on the words *apartment* and *mime* are key to getting the humor in the jokes, and both require a somewhat sophisticated understanding of the inappropriate behavioral absurdities described. The following riddle similarly requires a quick connection between pun and history: What do you call it when someone throws a bomb into a French kitchen? Linoleum blown apart.

And only an educator would truly appreciate the comment a teacher once made to me that she wanted to die during an inservice workshop because the transition from life to death would be so subtle.

The arts similarly are a marvelous vehicle for exploring what's appropriate and inappropriate because the arts don't try to solve problems with a simple veridical (true/false) solution. Rather, they use pretend situations that are removed from reality to explore such dichotomies as right/wrong, fair/unfair, beautiful/ugly, and interesting/ boring. The arts don't merely depict something, but they metaphorically analyze it in a way that forces folks to find an equivalent issue in their own life. So as you use the arts (and humor) in helping students to understand issues in classroom management, help them to get as close as they can to the subtleties in the discrepancies that define the issue they're trying to understand and resolve.

In the End

Appropriate behavior is a two-sided coin. What do students have a right to expect from educators? What do educators have a right to expect from students?

Reasonable Student Expectations. Chapter 1 began with John Dewey's strong belief that democratic values must permeate schools that hope to educate citizens capable of functioning effectively in a democratic society. These would include (1) constitutional rights to free speech, privacy, and due process; (2) legal rights to a quality education in a safe, nonrestrictive, nonharassing environment; and (3) a policy of distributed participation in decision making, such as with classroom management issues and procedures. The courts have generally given schools some slack when educators unilaterally prohibit controversial behaviors they believe will reduce educational effectiveness, but it's not a good idea to lean on the constitutional and fundamental human rights of students in doing it. Even if a school wins in court, it tends to lose support in the community and often ends up the focus of ridicule.

Students also have a right to expect that educators will operate with the dignity and integrity of adult behavior but at a personally pleasant level that's appropriate to someone who is working with immature students. Students further have a right to teachers who understand the curriculum and have mastered basic instructional and management skills. We can probably reduce it all down to an expectation that teachers should be interesting, curious, and fair adults. The old adage is that the quantity of student misbehavior is directly related to the quality of the teacher's behavior. Well, OK, plus a lot of other things that teachers can't control. The reality, though, is that the only thing we can really control is the quality of our own classroom behavior and instruction—and we ought to take care of our part of the equation, despite what others might do.

Teachers who constantly complain about all the things that students can't and won't do are like custodians who complain about dirty floors. Dirty floors help to define their job. Similarly, the considerable inabilities of students define a teacher's job. If you don't appreciate student ignorance, eradicate it!

This book has strongly argued that collaborative classroom management ought to be an important part of the curriculum. The classroom management curriculum best functions in an exploratory environment that enthusiastically involves students in the observation, study, and analysis of their own behavior (and its underlying biological substrate) and then encourages them to creatively explore new ways of solving practical classroom management problems. Proposed solutions don't always have to work (the problem that a class is trying to solve is an example of something that's not working). If a proposal doesn't work, try something else. It's the exploratory environment of shared management that's the important element. It's process, not product.

Reasonable School Expectations. What should educators expect of students? They're personally immature and will communicate it in many amazing ways. They come with a stunning array of immature cognitive systems and an innate drive to further develop them—in or out of school, whoever makes the best offer. They truly want to develop friendships, but their immature social skills often thwart their best-laid plans. Their out-of-school family and community life strongly affects their school life. They depend heavily on adults to support them, and so they're appropriately concerned when the support is weak or absent, and school work moves well down the priority list at such times. They grouse a lot about school and its expectations, but most (at least secretly) like to go to school because that's where their friends are.

Teachers have a right to expect that students will help to maintain an environment that's conducive to learning and that they will work to learn the things that the community deems important. That's not an unreasonable expectation. Students aren't currently productive citizens, but our society has a right to insist that they master the minimum knowledge and skills required of productive adults, whether they like it or not. We're a social species, so individuals don't have a right to expect that others will support them throughout their lifetime. Teachers have a right to be quite assertive about this.

The preceding paragraph isn't an authoritarian dictum in a classroom in which students are encouraged to participate in solving their own management issues. Students will come to understand it for what it is—a clear delineation of tasks and responsibilities but a shared commitment to collaborate.

However we manage a classroom, it's almost impossible to objectively define the subjective concept of *culturally appropriate.* Culturally appropriate is something we constantly negotiate in our own life and in our interactions with others. We expect others to operate within our idea of a normal range—behavior that's comfortable, familiar—and yet most of us constantly explore life beyond our normal range to see how it is.

People who live in big cities vacation in rural areas, and vice versa. People climb mountains and take tour boats to the Antarctica but have no plans to settle there. The success of such magazines as *People* suggests that we have a voyeuristic tendency to look in on (and perhaps cluck our tongues at) the behavior of celebrities—people who are well known for their well-knownness, as Andy Warhol once put it. We further peek in on TV shows that exploit the personal problems of noncelebrities who will claw and fight on nationwide TV for 10 minutes of celebrity, and like the raucous studio audience that loudly indicates who they believe acted appropriately and inappropriately, we also make our own private judgments. We read the advice columns, letters to the editor, film reviews, and editorial columnists and then privately determine our own beliefs about what's appropriate and inappropriate. We get involved with election campaigns and local issues and then privately vote our own opinion on what is appropriate and inappropriate. It's difficult to think of a day when we adults don't get involved with these kinds of decisions hundreds of times.

So what's the normal range, and where are the edges that lead to abnormality? Over time, students discover their teacher's beliefs about the point at which behavior is unacceptable, and they'll realize that on some days the acceptable range is narrower or broader than on other days. But they'll finally get a handle on the fluctuating realities of their teacher's expectations, and then a substitute will show up one morning, and the first thing the class will have to do without the help of their regular teacher is to discover all over again the point at which normal behavior becomes abnormal.

References and Supplementary Readings

Andreasen, N. (2001). *Brave new brain: Conquering mental illness in the era of the genome.* New York: Oxford University Press.

Barkow, J., Cosmides, L., & Tooby, J. (1992). *The adapted mind: Evolutionary Psychology and the generation of culture.* New York: Oxford University Press.

Blackmore, S. (1999). *The meme machine.* New York: Oxford University Press.

Bower, B. (1995). Criminal intellects: Researchers look at why lawbreakers often brandish low I.Q.'s. *Science News, 147*(15): 232-239.

Butterworth, B. (1999). *What counts: How every brain is hardwired for math.* New York: Free Press.

Calvin, W. (1996a). *The cerebral code: Thinking a thought in the mosaics of the mind.* Cambridge: MIT Press.

Calvin, W. (1996b). *How brains think: Evolving intelligence: Then and now.* New York: Basic Books.

Carter, R. (1998). *Mapping the mind.* Berkeley: University of California Press.

Clark, A. (1998). *Being there: Putting brain, body, and the world together again.* Cambridge: MIT Press.

Cobb, K. (2002). Sleepy heads. *Science News, 162*(3), 38.

Coccaro, E. (1995, January). Biology of aggression. *Scientific American Science and Medicine,* pp. 38-47.

Corballis, M. (2002). *From hand to mouth: The origins of language.* Princeton, NJ: Princeton University Press.

Damasio, A. (1999). *The feeling of what happens: Body and emotion in the making of consciousness.* New York: Harcourt Brace.

Davis, J. (1997). *Mapping the mind: The secrets of the human brain and how it works.* Secaucus, NJ: Birch Lane Press.

Dawkins, R. (1989a). *A river out of Eden: A Darwinian view of life.* New York: Basic Books.

Dawkins, R. (1989b). *The selfish gene.* New York: Oxford University Press.

Dehaene, S. (1997). *The number sense: How the mind creates mathematics.* New York: Oxford University Press.

DeWaal, F. (1996). *Good natured: The origins of right and wrong in humans and other animals.* Cambridge: Harvard University Press.

Dewey, J. (1938). *Experience and education.* New York: Macmillan.

Diamond, M., & Hopson, J. (1998). *The magic trees of the mind: How to nurture your child's intelligence, creativity, and healthy emotions from birth through adolescence.* New York: Dutton.

Dozier, R. (1998). *Fear itself: The origin and nature of the powerful emotion that shapes our lives and our world.* New York: St. Martin's.

Dubin, M. (2002). *How the brain works.* Williston, VT: Blackwell.

Edelman, G. (1992). *Bright air, brilliant fire: On the matter of the mind.* New York: Basic Books.

Elbert, T., Pantex, C., Weinbruch, C., Rockstroh, B., & Taub, E. (1995). Increased cortical representations on the fingers of the left hand in string players. *Science, 270,* 305-306.

Ellison, L. (2001). *The personal intelligences: Promoting social and emotional learning.* Thousand Oaks, CA: Corwin Press.

Fuller, R. (1995). Neural functions of serotonin. *Scientific American Science and Medicine, 2*(4), 48-52.

Gardner, H. (1983). *Frames of mind: The theory of multiple intelligences.* New York: Basic Books.

Gardner, H. (1998). A multiplicity of intelligences. *Scientific American Presents, 9*(4), 18-23.

Gardner, H. (1999). *The disciplined mind: What all students should understand.* New York: Simon & Schuster.

Gevins, A. (1997). What to do with your own personal brain scanner. In R. Solso (Ed.), *Mind and brain sciences in the 21st century* (pp. 111–125). Cambridge: MIT Press.

Goldberg, E. (2001). *The executive brain: Frontal lobes and the civilized mind.* New York: Oxford University Press.

Goleman, D. (1995). *Emotional intelligence: Why it can matter more than I.Q.* New York: Bantam.

Hobson, J. (1994). *The chemistry of conscious states: How the brain changes its mind.* Boston: Little, Brown.

Holmes, T., & Rahe, R. (1967). The Social Readjustment Rating Scale. *Journal of Psychosomatic Research, 11,* 213-218.

Jensen, E. (1998). *Teaching with the brain in mind.* Alexandria, VA: ASCD.

Johns, T. (1990). *With bitter herbs they shall eat it: Chemical ecology and the origins of human diet and medicine.* Tucson: University of Arizona Press.

Johnson, D. (1995). *Reducing school violence through conflict resolution.* Alexandria, VA: ASCD.

Kagan, J. (1994). *Galen's prophecy: Temperament in human nature.* New York: Basic Books.

Kagan, S. (1992). *Cooperative learning resources for teachers.* San Clemente, CA: Kagan.

Kandel, M., & Kandel, E. (1994). Flights of memory. *Discover Magazine, 15*(6), 32-38.

Kays, D. (1990). *A comparison of the attendance rates and patterns of fourth and fifth grade at-risk students in 27 elementary schools.* Unpublished doctoral dissertation, University of Oregon, Eugene.

Klawans, H. (1996). *Why Michael can't hit: And other tales of the neurology of sports.* New York: Freeman.

Kohn, A. (1996). *Beyond discipline: From compliance to community.* Alexandria, VA: ASCD.

LeDoux, J. (2002). *The synaptic self: How our brains become who we are.* New York: Viking.

Lyons, M. (1977). *An inquiry into sixth grader pupils' responses to in-class waiting.* Unpublished doctoral dissertation, University of Oregon, Eugene.

Meltzoff, A., & Prinz, W. (2002). *The imitative mind: Development, evolution, and brain bases.* Cambridge, UK: Cambridge University Press.

Motluk, A. (2001). Read my mind. *New Scientist, 169*(2275), 22-26.

Nesse, R., & Williams, G. (1994). *Why we get sick: The new science of Darwinian medicine.* New York: Random House.

Niehoff, D. (1999). *The biology of violence.* New York: Free Press.

Parasuraman, R. (1998). *The attentive brain.* Cambridge: MIT Press.

Perkins, D. (1995). *Outsmarting I.Q.: The emerging science of learnable intelligence.* New York: Free Press.

Pert, C. (1997). *The molecules of emotion: Why you feel the way you feel.* New York: Scribner's.

Pinker, S. (1997). *How minds work.* New York: Norton.

Posner, M., & Raichle, M. (1994). *Images of mind.* New York: Freeman.

Premack, D., & Premack, A. (2003). *Original intelligence: Unlocking the mystery of who we are.* New York: McGraw-Hill.

Profet, M. (1992). Pregnancy sickness as adaptation: A deterrent to maternal ingestion of teratogens. In J. H. Barkow (Ed.), *The adapted mind* (pp. 327-365). New York: Oxford University Press.

Provine, R. (2001). *Laughter: A scientific investigation.* New York: Viking.

Ramachandran, V. S. (2000). *Mirror neurons* [Online]. Retrieved from www.edge.org/documents/archive/edge69.html (See also R. Sylwester's column on mirror neurons in *Brain Connection,* August 2002 [Online]. Retrieved from www.brainconnection. com)

Ratey, J. (2001). *A user's guide to the brain.* New York: Pantheon.

Restak, R. (2002). *The secret life of the brain.* Washington, DC: Joseph Henry Press.

Ridley, M. (1996). *The origins of virtue: Human instincts and the evolution of cooperation.* New York: Viking.

Rousell, L. (1992). *A comprehensive examination of grief themes in young children's books.* Unpublished doctoral dissertation, University of Oregon, Eugene.

Rymer, R. (1993). *Genie: An abused child's flight from silence.* New York: HarperCollins.

Sapolsky, R. (1997). Testosterone rules. *Discover Magazine, 18,* 45-50.

Sapolsky, R. (1998). *Why zebras don't get ulcers: An updated guide to stress, stress-related diseases, and coping.* New York: Freeman.

Sapolsky, R. (1999). Stress and your shrinking brain. *Discover Magazine, 20*(3), 116-122.

Schwartz, J. & Begley, S. (2002). *The mind and the brain: Neuroplasticity and the power of mental force.* New York: Harper Collins.

Scientific Learning Corporation. (1997). Fast ForWord [computer software]. Berkeley, CA: Author.

Siegal, D. (1999). *The developing mind: Towards a neurobiology of interpersonal experience.* New York: Guilford.

Sousa, D. (2001). *How the brain learns.* Thousand Oaks, CA: Corwin Press.

Sternberg, R. (1985). *Beyond I.Q.: A triarchic theory of human intelligence.* New York: Cambridge University Press.

Stevens, J., & Goldberg, D. (2001). *For the learner's sake: Brain-based instruction for the 21st century.* Tucson: Zephyr Press.

Sylwester, R. (1997a). Bioelectronic learning: The effects of electronic media on a developing brain. *Technos Quarterly, 6*(2), 19-23.

Sylwester, R. (1997b, February). The neurobiology of self-esteem and aggression. *Educational Leadership,* pp. 75-79.

Sylwester, R. (1998a, February). Art for the brain's sake. *Educational Leadership,* pp. 31-35.

Sylwester, R. (1998b, January). The brain revolution. *The School Administrator, 55*(1), 6-8.

Sylwester, R. (1995). *A celebration of neurons: An educator's guide to the human brain.* Alexandria, VA: ASCD.

Sylwester, R. (1999). In search of the roots of adolescent aggression. *Educational Leadership, 57*(1), 65-69.

Sylwester, R. (2001). Genetics: The new staff development challenge. *Educational Leadership, 59*(2), 17-19.

Sylwester, R., & Margulies, N. (1998). *Discover your brain* (A two-part instructional program on Emotion/Attention and on Memory for Middle School Students). Tucson: Zephyr Press.

Volavka, J. (1995). *The neurobiology of violence.* Washington, DC: American Psychiatric Press.

Walker, H. (1998). First step to prevent antisocial behavior. *Teaching Exceptional Children, 30*(4), 16-19.

Walker, H., & Sylwester, R. (1998). Reducing students' refusal and resistance. *Teaching Exceptional Children, 30*(6), 52-57.

Werner, E., & Smith, R. (1992). *Overcoming the odds: High risk children from birth to adulthood.* Ithaca, NY: Cornell University Press.

Wilson, E. O. (1998). *Consilience: The unity of knowledge.* New York: Knopf.

Wolfe, P. (2001). *Brain matters: Translating research into classroom practice.* Alexandria, VA: ASCD.

Wright, K. (2002). Times of our lives. *Scientific American, 287*(3), 58-65.

Wright, R. (1995, March 13). The biology of violence. *The New Yorker,* pp. 66-77.

Wurtman, J., & Suffes, S. (1996). *The serotonin solution: The potent brain chemical that can help you to stop bingeing, lose weight, and feel great.* New York: Fawcett Columbine.

Index

**CORWIN
PRESS**

The Corwin Press logo—a raven striding across an open book—represents the happy union of courage and learning. We are a professional-level publisher of books and journals for K-12 educators, and we are committed to creating and providing resources that embody these qualities. Corwin's motto is "Success for All Learners."